A Camaraderie *of*

Confidence

Books by John Piper

Battling Unbelief

Bloodlines: Race, Cross, and the Christian

Brothers, We Are Not Professionals

Contending for Our All (Swans 4)

The Dangerous Duty of Delight

The Dawning of Indestructible Joy

Desiring God

Does God Desire All to Be Saved?

Don't Waste Your Life

Fifty Reasons Why Jesus Came to Die

Filling Up the Afflictions of Christ (Swans 5)

Finally Alive

Five Points

Future Grace

God Is the Gospel

God's Passion for His Glory

A Godward Heart

A Godward Life

The Hidden Smile of God (Swans 2)

A Hunger for God

The Legacy of Sovereign Joy (Swans 1)

Lessons from a Hospital Bed

Let the Nations Be Glad!

A Peculiar Glory

The Pleasures of God

The Roots of Endurance (Swans 3)

Seeing and Savoring Jesus Christ

Seeing Beauty and Saying Beautifully (Swans 6)

Spectacular Sins

The Supremacy of God in Preaching

A Sweet and Bitter Providence

Taste and See

Think

This Momentary Marriage

What Jesus Demands from the World

What's the Difference?

When I Don't Desire God

THE SWANS ARE NOT SILENT

Book Seven

A CAMARADERIE *of* CONFIDENCE

The Fruit of Unfailing Faith in the Lives of
CHARLES SPURGEON, GEORGE MÜLLER, AND HUDSON TAYLOR

JOHN PIPER

CROSSWAY®
WHEATON, ILLINOIS

A *Camaraderie of Confidence: The Fruit of Unfailing Faith in the Lives of Charles Spurgeon, George Müller, and Hudson Taylor*

Copyright © 2016 by Desiring God Foundation

Published by Crossway
    1300 Crescent Street
    Wheaton, Illinois 60187

Cover image: Howell Golson

First printing 2016

Printed in the United States of America

Trade paperback ISBN: 978-1-4335-5185-7
ePub ISBN: 978-1-4335-5188-8
PDF ISBN: 978-1-4335-5186-4
Mobipocket ISBN: 978-1-4335-5187-1

Library of Congress Cataloging-in-Publication Data

Names: Piper, John, 1946– author.
Title: A camaraderie of confidence: the fruit of unfailing faith in the lives of Charles Spurgeon, George Müller, and Hudson Taylor / John Piper.
Description: Wheaton : Crossway, 2016. | Series: The swans are not silent; 7 | Includes bibliographical references and index.
Identifiers: LCCN 2015037473 (print) | LCCN 2016002501 (ebook) | ISBN 9781433551857 (hc) | ISBN 9781433551864 (pdf) | ISBN 9781433551871 (mobi) | ISBN 9781433551888 (epub)
Subjects: LCSH: Christian biography—England. | Spurgeon, C. H. (Charles Haddon), 1834–1892. Müller, George, 1805–1898. | Taylor, James Hudson, 1832–1905. | England—Church history—19th century.
Classification: LCC BR1700.3 .P5548 2016 (print) | LCC BR1700.3 (ebook) | DDC 274.20092/2—dc23
LC record available at http://lccn.loc.gov/2015037473

Crossway is a publishing ministry of Good News Publishers.

LB		24	23	22	21	20	19	18	17	16
15	14	13	12	11	10	9	8	7	6	5	4	3	2	1

To the Global Partners
who have gone out from Bethlehem Baptist Church
for the sake of the Name

CONTENTS

Preface 9

Introduction: A Camaraderie of Confidence in the Mighty
    Goodness of God 13

1   Charles Spurgeon: Preaching through Adversity 33

2   George Müller: A Strategy for Showing God—
    Simple Faith, Sacred Scripture, Satisfaction in God 63

3   Hudson Taylor: An Enduring and Expansive Enjoyment
    of Union with Jesus Christ 85

Conclusion 105

Index of Scriptures 111

Index of Persons 113

Index of Subjects 115

PREFACE

This is book seven in the series of biographical studies called The
Swans Are Not Silent. The series title comes from the story of Augustine's retirement as the bishop of Hippo in North Africa in AD 426.
His successor, Eraclius, contrasted himself with Augustine by saying, "The cricket chirps, the swan is silent."[1] It was humble. But in a
profound sense, it was untrue. Augustine became probably the most
influential theologian in the history of the Christian church. The swan
was not—and is not—silent.

So when I say "The Swans Are Not Silent," I mean: there are voices
from church history that are still heard, and should be heard, in the
ongoing history of the church. My hope is that this series will give
voice to some of these swans. In this volume, the swans are Charles
Spurgeon, the greatest preacher of the nineteenth century; George
Müller, the great lover of orphans and supporter of missions; and
Hudson Taylor, the founder of the China Inland Mission. Some of the
things that bind them together are that they were all contemporaries,
based in England, knew each other, encouraged each other, and took
inspiration from each other's lives.

When one reads the history of evangelicalism in the nineteenth
century,[2] and reads the lives of Spurgeon, Müller, and Taylor against
that backdrop, one can't help but see that they were part of something
much bigger than themselves. The waves of the Great Awakenings

---

[1] Peter Brown, *Augustine of Hippo* (Berkeley, CA: University of California Press, 1969), 408.
[2] The stories of the first and second halves of the century are told respectively by John Wolffe, *The Expansion of Evangelicalism: The Age of Wilberforce, More, Chalmers and Finney* (Downers Grove, IL: InterVarsity Press, 2007), and David W. Bebbington, *The Dominance of Evangelicalism: The Age of Spurgeon and Moody* (Downers Grove, IL: InterVarsity Press, 2005).

had broken over Britain and America, and remarkable advances were happening in the growth of the Christian movement. The Awakening of 1859 was sending its ripple effects from Canada to Ireland, Scotland, Wales, and England. The time was right for these three evangelicals, and they were both very like and very unlike their era. But in their similarities and distinctives, they were bound together with each other and with the evangelical movement. They may seem like meteors in their own right. But they were part of a constellation.

Similarly, in our own day, I feel woven together with many people in all the undertakings of my life. For example, when it came to researching the relationships between Spurgeon, Müller, and Taylor, there was a community of friends and scholars I could turn to who love these heroes. Here at Desiring God, content strategist and staff writer Tony Reinke spearheaded the effort to gather insights about how these "swans" related to each other. With his help, I reached out to Michael Haykin, professor of church history and biblical spirituality at Southern Baptist Theological Seminary; Thomas Nettles, recently retired professor of historical theology at Southern; Christian George, assistant professor of historical theology and curator of the Spurgeon Library at Midwestern Baptist Theological Seminary; and Jim Elliff, president of Christian Communicators Worldwide. Mark Noll directed me to the work of Alvyn Austin on the history of the China Inland Mission.[3] These friends responded with generous pointers that have shaped this book.

Of course, it almost goes without saying that I am indebted to dozens of other researchers and writers who over the years have studied and written about Spurgeon, Müller, and Taylor. I did not have access to any original sources that are not available to everybody. Whatever is fresh about the stories I tell is not owing to fresh sources, but fresh reading and thinking and comparing. So I have a great debt to the

---

[3] Alvyn Austin, *China's Millions: The China Inland Mission and Late Qing Society, 1832–1905* (Grand Rapids, MI: Eerdmans, 2007).

biographies and articles in which others have presented the facts of these men's lives.

A new development in my own indebtedness to the community of scholars and students of history and Scripture is the extraordinary possibilities that now exist with Logos Bible Software (now part of Faithlife). Logos has made available the works of Spurgeon, Müller, and Taylor electronically so that one can search them for names and words and phrases almost instantaneously. Thus, it is possible in a matter of seconds to see every place where Spurgeon, for example, in his sixty-three volumes of sermons, refers to Müller or Taylor. You can easily imagine the possibilities of looking up terms and phrases. I am deeply thankful for how responsive Logos has been to requests I have made for the addition of certain works to its already massive library of electronic books.

Closer to home, as always, my life is freed and encouraged for the work of writing by Marshall Segal and David Mathis, both writers and editors for Desiring God. They provide the practical, critical, and visionary help to make me productive. They are part of the web of relationships without which my life would be a drab and lonely affair.

Saying thank you for the help I received on this book is complicated by the fact that the writing of it spans twenty years. The first draft of the Spurgeon section was written in 1995. The main constant relationships in my life over those years are Jesus and my wife, Noël. There are others, but without these—no books. God has been kind to me. When I ponder the relationships among Spurgeon, Müller, and Taylor, I feel a special gratitude for the matrix of relationships in my life. Only God knows what life would have been if anyone were missing.

I pray now that these three "swans" will sing their way into your life. What they have to teach us and show us about the camaraderie of confidence in God, in all his goodness, glory, and power, is enormous. Let them lead you into a life of greater faith and joy and radical commitment to Christ's mission in this world.

It was George Müller who said it, with that holy blessed life of faith at the back of every word; and I was like a child, sitting at a tutor's feet, to learn of him.

Charles Spurgeon

No mission now existing has so fully our confidence and good wishes as the work of Mr. Hudson Taylor in China. It is conducted on those principles of faith in God which most dearly commend themselves to our innermost soul. The man at the head is "a vessel fit for the Master's use." His methods of procedure command our veneration.

Charles Spurgeon

INTRODUCTION

A Camaraderie of Confidence in the
Mighty Goodness of God

INDIGENOUS, TRANSFORMING EXILES

In some ways Charles Spurgeon, "the greatest preacher" of the nineteenth century,[1] and George Müller, who cared for thousands of orphans, and Hudson Taylor, who founded the China Inland Mission, were men of their amazing age. In other ways, they were exiles on the earth—a camaraderie of confidence in something beyond this world. This is not an exceptional statement, since the same could be said of almost every Christian who believes the gospel and wants to serve the temporal and eternal needs of his fellow man.

The roots of this simple observation are in the Bible. On the one hand, we are told that Christians are "sojourners and exiles" (1 Pet. 2:11) whose "citizenship is in heaven" (Phil. 3:20). On the other hand, the apostle Paul said, "I have become all things to all people, that by all means I might save some" (1 Cor. 9:22). Not surprisingly, fruitful Christians are people of their age, and yet also people out of step with their age.

It is the divine genius of Christianity that incarnation and transformation are built into the very nature of the coming of Christ. He was one of us. And he was infinitely different from us. He fit in. But

---

[1] David W. Bebbington, *The Dominance of Evangelicalism: The Age of Spurgeon and Moody* (Downers Grove, IL: InterVarsity Press, 2005), 40, 267.

he changed everything. Therefore, Christianity spreads in the same way—from age to age and from culture to culture. It adapts to culture and it alters culture. It puts on the culture's clothes and changes the culture's heart. Then that heart-change circles back around to the clothes—and everything.

Andrew Walls, a former missions professor at the University of Edinburgh, calls these two truths the "indigenizing principle" and the "pilgrim principle." Both are rooted in the heart of the Christian faith—the doctrines of justification and sanctification. "On the one hand, it is the essence of the Gospel that God accepts us as we are, on the ground of Christ's work, alone, not on the ground of what we have become or are trying to become."[2] That means we bring our culturally conditioned ways of life into Christ.

But as Walls points out:

> [There is] another force in tension with this indigenizing principle, and this also is equally of the Gospel. Not only does God in Christ take people as they are: He takes them in order to transform them into what He wants them to be. . . . The Christian inherits the pilgrim principle, which whispers to him that he has no abiding city and warns him that to be faithful to Christ will put him out of step with his society; for that society never existed, in East or West, ancient time or modern, which could absorb the word of Christ painlessly into its system.[3]

MEN OF THEIR AGE

Spurgeon, Müller, and Taylor were clearly nineteenth-century men. Müller's life spanned the century (1805–1898). Spurgeon was cut down early by gout and Bright's disease at the age of fifty-seven (1834–1892). Taylor died five years into the twentieth century (1832–1905). But what made them men of their age was not merely their dates. They

---

[2] Andrew Walls, *The Missionary Movement in Christian History: Studies in the Transmission of Faith* (Maryknoll, NY: Orbis Books, 2001), 7.
[3] Ibid., 8.

were part of a great surge politically, industrially, and religiously. One could not live in the nineteenth century and fail to be affected by some of the biggest changes in the history of the world.

CITIZENS OF A GREAT EMPIRE

All three of these men were part of British culture, though Müller was born in Prussia and immigrated at the age of twenty-four. That meant that they were a part of an empire at the peak of its influence. There was only one monarch from 1837 to the end of the century, Queen Victoria—it was the Victorian Age. This stability was matched by a half-century of peace from 1850 onward. Globally, "Britain was at the height of its worldwide prestige."[4]

The most prominent statesman of the mid-century, Lord Palmerston, expressed the significance of the British Empire to the effect that "just as anyone in the ancient world could announce that he was a Roman citizen and the might of Rome's Empire would protect him, so Britain's authority would shield all who could claim to be subjects of the crown wherever they might be."[5]

FIRST MEMBERS OF THE MODERN WORLD

The Industrial Revolution and the age of invention were sweeping Britain into the modern world. In 1851, London hosted the Great Exhibition, with many new products on display. "But the overriding purpose was to celebrate the technical expertise of Britain, the first country to industrialize."[6] Between 1852 and 1892, the production of cotton in Britain tripled. The production of coal increased from 60 million tons in 1851 to 219 million tons fifty years later. It was the same in the United States. Coal production in that period jumped from 7 million to 268 million tons.

Railroads expanded dramatically. Steamships largely replaced

---

[4] Bebbington, *The Dominance of Evangelicalism*, 14.
[5] Cited in ibid., 13.
[6] Ibid., 17.

sailing vessels. This was the age of Thomas Edison and Alexander Graham Bell, both born in 1847. Electric lights, radio, the telephone, and other inventions were transforming life across the world. Patterns of life common for millennia were giving way to a new world.

Medical discoveries abounded. "In Britain over seventy special hospitals were founded between 1800 and 1860. . . . Among the drugs isolated, concocted, or discovered between 1800 and 1840 were morphine, quinine, atropine, digitalin, codeine, and iodine."[7] Along with industry and invention and discovery, prosperity followed. "For the first time many families had money to spend over and above what had to go toward subsistence."[8]

HEIRS OF THE GREAT AWAKENINGS

The first and second Great Awakenings had given a lasting impetus to world Christianity. Along with the population in general, the churches were expanding significantly. For example, between 1800 and 1850, the number of Methodists in England expanded from 96,000 to 518,000. The same was true for churches in Wales and Scotland. In the United States, it was equally dramatic. "Methodists increased from rather over 1,250,000 to about 5,500,000 members over the second half of the 19th century. Baptists rose from about 750,000 to about 4,500,000."[9]

More specifically, the Awakening of 1859 had a direct effect especially on Taylor's effort to reach China by founding the China Inland Mission. Alvyn Austin describes it:

> In 1859, while Hudson Taylor was still in China [on his first term before founding the CIM], a revival broke out in Northern Ireland that led to a religious movement so pivotal in British religious history that it came to be called the Revival or "Awakening of '59." . . . Although Taylor missed the first phase of the revival, he arrived in

---

[7] Bruce Haley, *The Healthy Body and Victorian Culture* (Cambridge, MA: Harvard University Press, 1987), n.p., cited at http://www.victorianweb.org/science/health/health12.html.
[8] Bebbington, *The Dominance of Evangelicalism*, 18.
[9] Ibid., 253.

Britain in time to reap its benefits. As J. Edwin Orr noted, "there is reason to believe that the whole [of the China Inland Mission's first] party [of 1866] was made up of converts and workers of the 1959 Awakening." . . . It is generally agreed that "something happened" in 1859–60, and that its ripples continued to reverberate for the rest of the century.[10]

It deserves mention in passing that this awakening was simultaneous with events that were hostile to the Christian faith. "In the secular realm, 1859 was equally momentous, with the publication of Darwin's *On the Origin of Species* and John Stuart Mill's essay *On Liberty*."[11] I mention this to show that we should be slow to assume that any particular cultural development (as in our own day, with the unraveling of the moral fabric of Western culture) should be seen as defining the trajectory of the future. God is always doing more than we know. Just when secular ways of seeing the world were intensifying, evangelical strength was also increasing.

At the end of the century, one estimate was that evangelicalism "represented the beliefs of 'not less, and probably many more, than sixty millions of avowed Christians in all parts of the world.'" David Bebbington endorses this estimate: "Including the converts of the missionary movement, [this] estimate was probably not far wrong."[12] Evangelicalism was the dominant form of Christianity, and Britain was the dominant empire.

THEY WERE EVANGELICALS

Bebbington has given one of the most compelling definitions of "evangelicalism" as a distinct movement rising out of the Great Awakening of the eighteenth century and continuing to this day. Spurgeon, Müller, and Taylor were supreme exemplars of this movement in their time.

---

[10] Alvyn Austin, *China's Millions: The China Inland Mission and Late Qing Society, 1832–1905* (Grand Rapids, MI: Eerdmans, 2007), 82–83, 85.

[11] Ibid., 82

[12] Bebbington, *The Dominance of Evangelicalism*, 263.

Bebbington argues that evangelicalism is a movement within Christianity marked by "crucicentrism, conversionism, Biblicism, and activism."[13] Or, more simply, "Bible, cross, conversion and activism were the characteristic themes of the evangelical movement."[14] Evangelicals "were stirred by the teaching of the *Scriptures*; they were eager to proclaim the message of *Christ crucified*; and they were unflagging in their quest for *conversions*. Hence they were dedicated *activists* in the spread of the gospel."[15]

The mark of evangelicalism that linked Spurgeon, Müller, and Taylor most clearly to their age was their activism. For all the depth of their theology and spirituality, these three giants were consummate doers. Bebbington notes, "The final mark of the evangelicals was an eagerness to be up and doing."[16]

ACTIVISM WAS IN THE AIR

Activism for social betterment was in the air. It was the air that evangelicals breathed. For example, one of the legacies of John Wesley (1703–1791) was a rule of his societies that Christians ought to avoid "soft and needless self-indulgence." In 1883, a New York Methodist newspaper asked what these words meant, and the *Christian Advocate* gave the official reply. The words covered "over-feeding, over-sleeping, over-clothing, idleness, pampering the body, living an easy, idle life, regarding work as an evil, and gratifying the appetites and passions."[17] We get the idea. The "idle life" is defective. Work is not evil. Self-indulgence is sin.

Social engagement for the betterment of the life of the oppressed was one pervasive expression of this activism. It may surprise some

---

[13] Ibid., 23.
[14] Ibid., 267.
[15] Ibid., 50 (emphasis added). To say it one more way, "evangelicalism typically chose to give prominence to conversion, the Bible, the cross and missionary activity. . . . These qualities renamed the defining features of evangelicalism down to the end of the century and beyond. . . . There were the typical emphases on the atoning work of Christ on the cross; the need for personal faith through conversion; the supreme value of the Bible; and the binding obligation of mission." Ibid., 22–23.
[16] Ibid., 36.
[17] Cited in ibid., 37.

people today, but evangelicals were at the cutting edge of this social activism for the sake of the poor. Bebbington gives abundant illustrations of the truth that "a plethora of churches and church-sponsored organizations throughout the English-speaking world tackled aspects of social destitution."[18]

The suspicion that many of us have inherited concerning the dilution of evangelism amid social concern was not true in general of nineteenth-century evangelicalism. "The typical disparagement by fundamentalists of concern for physical welfare was only just beginning as the 20th century opened. Down to 1900, what would later be called holistic mission was part of the agreed program of evangelicalism."[19] Thus, there were a "host of evangelicals of all denominations who attempted to redress the social conditions of Victorian Britain."[20]

One of the most prominent burdens felt by society and church was the plight of orphans. This plight was a common theme in the novels of nineteenth-century writer Charles Dickens (1812–1870). One feels the plight in the description of Oliver Twist: "He was badged and ticketed, and fell into his place at once—a parish child—the orphan of a workhouse—the humble, half-starved drudge—to be cuffed and buffeted through the world—despised by all, and pitied by none."[21]

Caring for Orphans by Faith

Ministers across Great Britain founded institutions to relieve the plight of the orphan. And that social work carried over into pressure for reform of working conditions and public treatment of the poor.[22] Müller was the most famous of the founders of orphanages, not because he was the only one doing it, but because of how he did it—namely, without asking for money or going into debt. Spurgeon,

---

[18] Ibid., 100–101.
[19] Ibid., 263.
[20] Ibid., 39.
[21] Charles Dickens, *Oliver Twist* (1838; repr., Ware, Hertfordshire, UK: Wordsworth, 1992), 5.
[22] Bebbington, *The Dominance of Evangelicalism*, 38.

in London, seventy miles from Bristol, where Müller's orphanages were, founded his own orphanages at Stockwell in 1867.

Taylor did not found a ministry directly for orphans, but the link with Müller's ministry is significant. Taylor's commitment to go to China as a missionary included his eagerness to be a blessing to the whole person, physical and spiritual. Hence, in 1851, on his nineteenth birthday, Taylor went to live with Dr. Robert Hardey in Hull as an apprentice in medicine.[23] While he was there, he became part of a Plymouth Brethren[24] fellowship where Müller was very highly esteemed.

Here is how Taylor's son, Frederick, recounts the importance of this connection with the Brethren and Müller, who himself was part of the Brethren:

> [Hudson] was hungry for the Word of God, and their preaching was for the most part a thoughtful exposition of its truths. He needed a fresh vision of eternal things, and the presence of Christ was often so real on these occasions that it was like heaven on earth to be among them. He was facing a difficult future, and they set before him an example of faith in temporal as well as spiritual things that surpassed his utmost thought. For this meeting was in close touch with George Müller of Bristol, whose work was even then assuming remarkable proportions. He had already hundreds of orphan children under his care, and was looking to the Lord for means to support a thousand. But this did not exhaust his sympathies. With a deep conviction that these are the days in which the Gospel must be preached "for a witness unto all nations," he

[23] Frederick Howard Taylor and Geraldine Taylor, *Hudson Taylor in Early Years: The Growth of a Soul* (Littleton, CO; Mississauga, ON; Kent, TN: OMF Books, 1995), 105.

[24] There is some ambiguity about the lifelong connection between the Plymouth Brethren and Taylor. The most extensive, scholarly study of the China Inland Mission and Taylor makes these observations: "Historians of the Brethren Movement claim Hudson Taylor as one of their own. As secretary Richard Hill whispered to Geraldine Guinness Taylor [Hudson Taylor's daughter-in-law], herself a second-generation Brethren: 'You know of course that the great majority of the earliest supporters were either or practically P.B.s [Plymouth Brethren].' Yet in her thirty books the word 'Brethren' never passed Mrs. Taylor's pen, hidden behind a cloud of euphemisms like 'chapel' and 'meeting.' A. J. Broomhall went to great lengths to deny the 'false label' that Taylor was connected with the Plymouth Brethren, that is, John Nelson Darby's Exclusives who practiced second-degree separation, which Taylor 'repudiated,' as well as the equally 'false label' that Taylor was a 'Baptist.' Broomhall did acknowledge that 'the non-sectarian, trans-denominational practices and principles of China Inland Mission . . . owed much' to the non-Plymouth or Open Brethren, like Berger, Grattan Guinness, and the Howard family." Austin, *China's Millions*, 94.

sustained in whole or part many missionaries, and was engaged in circulating the Scriptures far and wide in Roman Catholic as well as heathen lands. All this extensive work, carried on by a penniless man through faith in God alone, with no appeals for help or guarantee of stated income, was a wonderful testimony to the power of "effectual, fervent prayer." As such it made a profound impression upon Hudson Taylor, and encouraged him more than anything else could have in the pathway he was about to enter.[25]

So even though Taylor did not found an orphanage the way Müller and Spurgeon did, he was inspired by such work and in his own way became no less an activist, mobilizing thousands of missionaries for China—which to this day is transforming the way the Chinese think about children.

THE PERVASIVENESS OF PRACTICALITY

Of course, Spurgeon's orphanage was the tip of the iceberg of his activism. By the time he was fifty years old, he had founded, or was overseeing, sixty-six organizations. Lord Shaftesbury commented that this was a "a noble career of good . . . for the benefit of mankind."[26]

It would be a huge mistake to describe Spurgeon's activism as if he were not a man of profound personal faith and deep reliance on the Lord, with powerful capacities for enjoying the beauties of Christ and his world. We must get out of our heads entirely, when thinking of Spurgeon, Müller, and Taylor, that their activism was like the pragmatic activism of some today, who replace piety and prayer and meditation and worship with endless work. As will become clear in the chapters to follow, all of these men were mystics in their own way. That is, each had a profound, heartfelt, personal relationship with the living Christ.

Nevertheless, one cannot miss the pragmatic cast that colors even the most spiritual acts of Spurgeon. This is strikingly evident in his own words about prayer:

---

[25] Taylor and Taylor, *Hudson Taylor in Early Years*, 111–13.
[26] Cited in Arnold Dallimore, *Spurgeon* (Chicago: Moody Press, 1984), 173.

> When I pray, I like to go to God just as I go to a bank clerk when I have [a] cheque to be cashed. I walk in, put the cheque down on the counter, and the clerk gives me my money, I take it up, and go about my business. I do not know that I ever stopped in a bank five minutes to talk with the clerks; when I have received my change I go away and attend to other matters. That is how I like to pray; but there is a way of praying that seems like lounging near the mercy seat as though one had no particular reason for being found there.[27]

Again, it would be a caricature to take from these words the notion that Spurgeon did not believe in the sweetness of enjoying the presence of Christ in meditation and prayer. But one can hardly imagine someone talking like this three hundred years earlier. We are all profoundly shaped by the way the Holy Spirit meets us in our own age.

MODERN MAVERICKS

Part of the spirit of activism that was woven into the fabric of evangelicalism and into the expansive nineteenth-century ethos was a measure of pragmatic individualism. Spurgeon, Müller, and Taylor exploited this freedom to the full. I am not referring to a crass pragmatism that compromises biblical principles for the sake of measurable results. Almost the opposite. I am referring to a willingness to adjust inherited ways and traditions to put personal biblical convictions to practical use. If that makes one a maverick, so be it. Hence the individualism.

Bebbington points out how prevalent this spirit of pragmatic, can-do individualism was in the age of Spurgeon, Müller, and Taylor, in both Britain and America:

> The strength and number of para-church organizations—at the time called benevolent associations in America—is a sign of the

---

[27]Cited in Erroll Hulse and David Kingdon, eds., *A Marvelous Ministry: How the All-Round Ministry of Charles Haddon Spurgeon Speaks to Us Today* (Ligonier, PA: Soli Deo Gloria , 1993), 46–47.

same spirit of adapting church life to contemporary requirements. The range of miscellaneous but vigorous groups was immense— including in England the Army Scripture Readers' Society, the Christian Vernacular Society for India, the Working Men's Lord's Day Rest Association and the Society for the Relief of Persecuted Jews. Evangelicalism characteristically spawned organizations beyond the control of strictly ecclesiastical bodies.[28]

Both Müller and Taylor were disillusioned with the existing organizations of the day. In another age, they might have simply adjusted and made the best of things through slow reform. But in the nineteenth century, one could actually dream of taking charge, creating a new institution, and running and funding it practically as one saw fit.

MÜLLER'S LARGE AND LIBERAL ENTREPRENEURIALISM

In Müller's case, the orphan work was only one branch of a larger organization that he founded in 1834 (the year Spurgeon was born) called the Scripture Knowledge Institution for Home and Abroad. Through this Institution, he lavished his generosity (and remarkable fund-raising skill) on other causes of the gospel. For example, Müller became the largest donor to Taylor's China Inland Mission:

> In its early years he kept the mission afloat. From the fragmentary financial records, Moira McKay has ascertained that Müller contributed one-third of the CIM's income between 1866 and 1871, a total of £780 to the general fund and £560 to individual missionaries; this does not include money he gave Hudson Taylor personally for his own use, nor the money he remitted directly to China.[29]

Müller was committed not only to his own ministries. His large and entrepreneurial heart had a wider kingdom focus. But it should be mentioned that, for all the wideness of his generosity, he never lost

---

[28] Bebbington, *The Dominance of Evangelicalism*, 145.
[29] Austin, *China's Millions*, 96.

his doctrinal bearings. There came a point, for example, when he withheld his contributions to Taylor's CIM until the resignation of a key leader who had come to embrace the view of annihilationism in place of the biblical view of hell as eternal, conscious torment.[30]

A. T. Pierson, Müller's authorized biographer, said Müller's Scripture Knowledge Institution "owed its existence to the fact that its founder devised large and liberal things for the Lord's cause."[31] Indeed, that banner could be waved over the lives of all three of these men: they "devised large and liberal things for the Lord's cause."

But the impetus for new ministries was not merely entrepreneurial. When asked why he did not use existing institutions, Müller answered that they were out of step with what he saw in the Scriptures. "We found, in comparing the then existing religious Societies with the word of God, that they departed so far from it, that we could not be united with them, and yet maintain a good conscience."[32] Specifically, he said, (1) they tended to be postmillennial, (2) too many unregenerate persons were involved in running them, (3) they asked unconverted people for money, (4) the rich and unregenerate even served on their boards, (5) they tended to look for persons of rank to lead them, and (6) they were willing to fund their ministries by going into debt.[33]

So Müller started his own agency and led it in the way he understood the Scriptures to teach. From this individual commitment and vision flowed enormous energy and fruit. Besides caring for more than ten thousand orphans in his lifetime, the Scripture Knowledge Institution spread day schools across continental Europe, eventually serving more than one hundred twenty-three thousand students.[34]

---

[30] Ibid., 190.
[31] Arthur T. Pierson, *George Müller of Bristol: His Life of Prayer and Faith* (Grand Rapids, MI: Kregel, 1999), 248. Originally published as "Authorized Memoir" (Old Tappan, NJ: Revell, 1899).
[32] George Müller, *A Narrative of Some of the Lord's Dealings with George Muller, Written by Himself, Jehovah Magnified. Addresses by George Muller Complete and Unabridged*, vol. 1 (Muskegon, MI: Dust and Ashes Publications, 2003), 80.
[33] Ibid., 80–81.
[34] George Müller, *Autobiography of George Müller, or A Million and a Half in Answer to Prayer*, comp. G. Fred Bergin (Denton, TX: Westminster Literature Resources, 2003), ix.

And the Institution was among the first to get behind Taylor's China Inland Mission when it was founded in 1865.

Taylor Follows Müller's Model

Taylor's decision to start his own foreign mission sending agency was similarly driven by his disillusionment with the way other societies were run. He had gone to China in 1853 with the Chinese Evangelisation Society. But within four years, he resigned because he disagreed with the policy of the society to borrow money to pay its bills. "The Society itself was in debt. The quarterly bills which I and others were instructed to draw were often met with borrowed money, and a correspondence commenced which terminated in the following year by my resigning from conscientious motives."[35] Eight years later, he founded the China Inland Mission on principles like those of Müller's Institution. We tell that story in chapter 3.

The Modern Mavericks Were Very Unmodern—No Debt!

This issue of debt, together with the readiness to trust God to meet practical needs, is an example of how their very individualism and pragmatic adaptability could put Spurgeon, Müller, and Taylor not only in step with the spirit of the age, but radically out of step with it. All three of them rejected debt as a way of running any Christian ministry. And in its place, Müller and Taylor put a "faith principle"[36] that meant they would look to God and never directly ask another person for money.

Müller's conscience was bound by Romans 13:8: "Owe no man any thing" (KJV). He said: "There is no promise that He will pay our debts,—the word says rather: 'Owe no man any thing.'"[37] He believed

---

[35] *The Works of J. Hudson Taylor* (Douglas Editions, 2009). Kindle edition, locations 1508–1510.
[36] Bebbington, *The Dominance of Evangelicalism*, 185–90, describes how this "faith principle" rose up in the nineteenth century and shaped most of the evangelical movement. "By 1900 Anglican evangelicals were predominantly Keswick in their spirituality, millennial in their view of the future and at least respectful toward the faith principle." Ibid., 259.
[37] Müller, *A Narrative*, vol. 1, 316.

deeply that this way of life was the duty of every Christian and called on believers to repent if any were in debt. "The Lord helping us, we would rather suffer privation, than contract debts. . . . May I entreat the believing reader, prayerfully to consider this matter; for I am well aware that many trials come upon the children of God, on account of not acting according to Rom. xiii. 8."[38]

Müller went so far as to refuse to pay the milkman weekly, but would only pay him daily.[39] He did pay his workers a salary, but only with the understanding that "if the Lord should not be pleased to send in the means at the time when their salary is due, I am not considered their debtor."[40]

Taylor was born the year that Müller founded his Scripture Knowledge Institution. In due time, the reputation of Müller's faith made a huge impact on Taylor. The obituary that Thomas Champness wrote for Taylor in 1905 shows the extent of Müller's influence:

> HUDSON TAYLOR is no more! A Prince of Israel has been gathered home. He died in China, the land he loved more than life. Now that he has gone we shall hear more of him. In his way he was as great a man as George Müller. Like him, he had more faith in God than man. The China Inland Mission, of which he was the founder, was run on similar lines to the Orphanage at Bristol. What the writer of these lines owes to Hudson Taylor will never be known.[41]

Under Taylor's leadership, the China Inland Mission was never in debt and never directly asked for money.

The influence of Müller on Taylor was direct from the first time that they met:

> Although Müller had given financial contributions to Taylor since 1857, they do not seem to have met until 1863, when Taylor took Wang Lae-djün to Bristol to sit at Müller's feet. . . . The grand

---

[38] Ibid., 62.
[39] Ibid., 169.
[40] Ibid., 256.
[41] *In Memoriam: J. Hudson Taylor* (London: Morgan & Scott, 1906), 102.

old man—he was nearing sixty, almost gaunt-looking, with a white beard and unruly hair—bequeathed two gifts to the young man. The first were his mottoes, which became the watchwords of the CIM: "Ebenezer" ("Hitherto hath the Lord helped us") and "Jehovah-Jireh" ("the Lord will provide"). Taylor transcribed them into Chinese, and printed them on the cover of every issue of *China's Millions*: *Yi-ben-yi-shi-er* and *Ye-he-hua-yi-la*. Müller's second gift was his system for divine bookkeeping: each donor was given a numbered receipt, which Müller published in consecutive order, anonymously, on regular occasions.[42]

Like Müller and Taylor, Spurgeon said he hated debt the way Martin Luther hated the pope. All the buildings he built were entered debt-free.[43] But it does not appear that he embraced the principle of not asking for funds the way Müller and Taylor did. The explanation seems plain enough. He was a pastor charged with preaching the Scriptures to his flock and applying it, not merely to parachurch organizations, but specifically to his people's relationships. One of those relationships was with the local church to which they belonged—the Metropolitan Tabernacle. If any text a pastor touches involves the teaching that the members of a church should sustain the church financially, then not only *may* the pastor exhort the people to give, he would be untrue to the text if he didn't.

Spurgeon loved Müller as a close comrade in ministry and as one of his heroes. He conversed with him often[44] and called him his "dear friend." Müller preached occasionally in Spurgeon's Metropolitan Tabernacle.[45] Spurgeon's praise for Müller was unparalleled for any man in his day. "I never heard a man who spoke more to my soul than

[42] Austin, *China's Millions*, 95–96.
[43] Eric W. Hayden, *Highlights in the Life of C. H. Spurgeon* (Pasadena, TX: Pilgrim Publications, 1990), 95.
[44] Müller shared Spurgeon's affection and recalled several conversations when Spurgeon was on vacation in Mentone, France. "At Mentone I enjoyed especially the intercourse I had with Mr. Spurgeon, with whom I spent repeatedly a considerable time." George Müller, *Autobiography of George Muller: A Million and a Half in Answer to Prayer* (London: J. Nisbet, 1914), 532.
[45] "On our way to Sunderland, I preached in the large Metropolitan Tabernacle for Mr. Spurgeon." Ibid., 526.

dear Mr. George Müller."[46] "I think, sometimes, that I would not mind changing places with George Müller for time and for eternity, but I do not know anybody else of whom I would say as much as that."[47]

Perhaps only slightly less was Spurgeon's admiration for Taylor. In the nature of the case, the relationship could not be as close, since Müller was only a few hours away in Bristol, while Taylor was often in China. Nevertheless, Spurgeon sang the praises of Taylor and the China Inland Mission:

> No mission now existing has so fully our confidence and good wishes as the work of Mr. Hudson Taylor in China. It is conducted on those principles of faith in God which most dearly commend themselves to our innermost soul. The man at the head is "a vessel fit for the Master's use." His methods of procedure command our veneration—by which we mean more than our judgment or our admiration; and the success attending the whole is such as cheers our heart and reveals the divine seal upon the entire enterprise.[48]

In other words, Spurgeon's unwillingness to trumpet the exact same funding strategy as Müller and Taylor did not diminish his affection and admiration and support for them. In fact, he admired their faith and their strategy

The Unifying Root of Renegade Finances

Why did Taylor and Müller adopt the pattern of not asking people directly for funds?[49]

Müller gave the clearest answer. And this answer shows how he and Spurgeon and Taylor were utterly out of step with their age.

---

[46]C. H. Spurgeon, *The Metropolitan Tabernacle Pulpit Sermons*, vol. 29 (London: Passmore & Alabaster, 1883), 389.

[47]C. H. Spurgeon, *The Metropolitan Tabernacle Pulpit Sermons*, vol. 49 (London: Passmore & Alabaster, 1903), 238.

[48]C. H. Spurgeon, *The Sword and the Trowel: 1869* (London: Passmore & Alabaster, 1869), 7.

[49]In the following chapters, it will become clear that while *direct* appeals for funds were not given, nevertheless both Müller and Taylor were vigilant about making use of the latest means of communicating to the world how God was meeting their needs, and thus *indirectly* communicated their needs and pulled at people's hearts.

Müller gave three reasons for establishing the orphan houses, and he gave them in the order of their importance in his mind:

> The three chief reasons for establishing an Orphan-House are: 1) That God may be glorified, should He be pleased to furnish me with the means, in its being seen that it is not a vain thing to trust in Him; and that thus the faith of His children may be strengthened. 2) The spiritual welfare of fatherless and motherless children. 3) Their temporal welfare.[50]

This is really astonishing, and a sure sign Müller was an exile and sojourner on the earth, with a true citizenship and treasure in heaven. The glory of God was preeminent for him, not the temporal welfare of the children. Caring for the children was the fruit of aiming to glorify God by showing him trustworthy. This is the highest and best gift he has for the children and for the world. Without this gift, all is in vain.

This is why Müller ran the orphanages the way he did—and in this goal, he was one with Spurgeon and Taylor. He wanted to give a living proof of the power and the trustworthiness of God, and the value of living by faith and prayer—without debt. When explaining why he never purchased anything for the orphan houses on credit, he said:

> The chief and primary object of the work was not the temporal welfare of the children, nor even their spiritual welfare (blessed and glorious as it is, and much as, through grace, we seek after it and pray for it); but the first and primary object of the work was: *To show before the whole world and the whole church of Christ, that even in these last evil days the living God is ready to prove Himself as the living God, by being ever willing to help, succour, comfort, and answer the prayers of those who trust in Him:* so that we need not go away from Him to our fellow-men, or to the ways of the world, seeing that He is both able and willing to supply us with all we can need in His service.[51]

---

[50] Müller, *A Narrative*, vol. 1, 103.
[51] Ibid., 317. See also 105.

Though there may have been minor differences in strategy and application, this passion for displaying God's faithfulness to the world bound these three friends together in their respective focuses of church (Spurgeon), orphan care (Müller), and world missions (Taylor).

INDIGENOUS PILGRIMS

Like every human being who lives in space and time—that is, in a particular culture and age—Charles Spurgeon, George Müller, and Hudson Taylor were shaped significantly by the explosive new world they inhabited. Their activism and individualism and pragmatism and resistance to elite privilege and identification with the common man (none of them had a theological degree) made them men of their age. Nevertheless, they were radically different from the unbelieving masses of their day.

What will become clear in the coming chapters is that, for all their differences, there was a profound camaraderie of confidence in God among them. They were indeed evangelical in their emphases on Scripture, the atoning work of Christ on the cross, the necessity of the new birth and conversion, and the resulting energy of activism and mission. But in each man's life, the suffering each would endure brought out an extraordinary confidence in the mighty goodness of God. Beneath all their talk of faith and the simplicity of trusting God to fulfill his promises for us in everyday life lay a massive vision of God's right and power to govern every detail of life, the evil and the good—with nothing able to stop him.

Taylor, who, among the three, was the least given to theological systematizing and labeling,[52] gave one of the strongest statements of this common conviction. When his wife Maria died after twelve years of marriage, Taylor was thirty-eight years old. He wrote to his mother,

---

[52]Spurgeon and Müller were self-confessed Calvinists. But in all the works by and about Taylor that I have seen, there is no clear statement on the matter. One pointer might be this excerpt from his commentary on the Song of Solomon: "In the little sister, as yet immature, may we not see the elect of GOD, given to CHRIST in GOD's purpose, but not yet brought into saving relation to Him?" Cited in J. Stuart Holden, "Foreword," in *Union and Communion; or, Thoughts on the Song of Solomon*, 3rd ed. (London: Morgan & Scott, 1914), 78.

"From my inmost soul I delight in the knowledge that God does or permits all things, and causes all things to work together for good to those who love Him."[53] Fourteen years later, at the age of fifty-two, he wrote, "So make up your mind that God is an infinite Sovereign, and has the right to do as He pleases with His own, and He may not explain to you a thousand things which may puzzle your reason in His dealings with you."[54]

Spurgeon and Müller said the same in similar contexts—Müller at the death of his wife, Spurgeon in the face of debilitating suffering. This was the uniting foundation of their camaraderie in confidence in the goodness, glory, and power of God. This would be the key to Spurgeon's powerful preaching through relentless adversity, Müller's unshakable satisfaction in God, and Taylor's enjoyment of his lasting union with Jesus Christ.

---

[53] Cited in Dr. and Mrs. Howard Taylor, *Hudson Taylor's Spiritual Secret*, Kindle edition (May 25, 2013), 163.
[54] Cited in Jim Cromarty, *It Is Not Death to Die* (Fearn, Ross-shire, Scotland: Christian Focus, 2008), 8.

Causeless depression cannot be reasoned with, nor can David's harp charm it away by sweet discoursings. As well fight with the mist as with this shapeless, undefinable, yet all-beclouding hopelessness . . .

The iron bolt which so mysteriously fastens the door of hope and holds our spirits in gloomy prison, needs a heavenly hand to push it back.

Charles Spurgeon

1

CHARLES SPURGEON

Preaching through Adversity

FOR PASTORS AND THE REST OF US

Everyone faces adversity and must find ways to persevere through the oppressing moments of life. Everyone must get up and walk through the routines of making breakfast and washing clothes and going to work and paying bills and discipling children. We must, in general, keep life going when our hearts are breaking.

But it's different with pastors—not *totally* different, but different. The heart is the instrument of our vocation. Charles Spurgeon said, "Ours is more than mental work—it is heart work, the labour of our inmost soul."[1] When a pastor's heart is breaking, therefore, he must labor with a broken instrument. Preaching is the pastor's main work, and preaching is heart work, not just mental work. The question becomes, then, not just how you keep living when the marriage is blank or when the finances don't reach or when the pews are bare and friends forsake you, but *How do you keep preaching?*

When the heart is overwhelmed, it's one thing to survive adversity; it is something entirely different to continue preaching Sunday after Sunday, month after month.

---

[1] Charles Spurgeon, *Lectures to My Students* (Grand Rapids, MI: Zondervan, 1972), 156.

Spurgeon said to the students of his Pastors' College: "One crushing stroke has sometimes laid the minister very low. The brother most relied upon becomes a traitor. . . . Ten years of toil do not take so much life out of us as we lose in a few hours by Ahithophel the traitor, or Demas the apostate."[2] The question for pastors is not, "How do you live through unremitting criticism and distrust and accusation and abandonment?"—but, "*How do you preach through it? How do you do heart work when the heart is under siege and ready to fall?*"

These are the uppermost questions for many pastors. Preaching great and glorious truth in an atmosphere that is not great and glorious is immensely difficult. To be reminded week in and week out that many people regard his preaching of the glory of God's grace as hypocrisy pushes a preacher not just into the hills of introspection, but sometimes to the precipice of self-extinction. I don't mean suicide—but something more complex. I mean the deranging inability to know any longer who you are.

What begins as a searching introspection for the sake of holiness and humility gradually leaves your soul, for various reasons, in a hall of mirrors. You look into one and you're short and fat; you look into another and you're tall and lanky; you look into another and you're upside down. Then the horrible feeling begins to break over you that you don't know who you are anymore. The center is not holding. If the center doesn't hold—if there is no fixed "I" able to relate to the fixed "thou" (namely, God), who is supposed to preach next Sunday?

When the apostle Paul said in 1 Corinthians 15:10, "By the grace of God I am what I am," he was saying something utterly essential for the survival of preachers in adversity. If the identity of the "I"—the "I" created by Christ and united to Christ, but still a human "I"—doesn't hold, there will be no more authentic preaching because there is no longer an authentic preacher. When the "I" is gone, there is only a collection of echoes.

---

[2] Ibid., 161.

Oh, how fortunate we are that we are not the first to face these things! I thank God for the healing history of the power of God in the lives of his saints and, in particular, for the life and ministry of Charles Spurgeon, who, for thirty-eight years at the New Park Street Chapel and the Metropolitan Tabernacle in London, modeled how to preach through adversity. And for those who have eyes to see, the lessons are not just for pastors, but for all of us.

PURITAN BEGINNINGS

Susannah Thompson, who became Spurgeon's wife for thirty-six years, was born in 1832, two years before her husband-to-be, and outlived him by eleven years. His life was enveloped in hers in more ways than one, as she served him, and the wider cause of Christ, even after she became an invalid twelve years into their marriage. She bore him two sons, twins, on September 20, 1856, Thomas and Charles Jr. Thomas would become the pastor of the Metropolitan Tabernacle after his father died, and Charles Jr. would take over the leadership of the Stockwell Orphanage that his father had founded.

George Müller was the great evangelical advocate for orphans in the nineteenth century, but Spurgeon, too, was passionate about this ministry. He started the Stockwell Orphanage in 1866, twelve years into his pastoral ministry in London. He loved to say, "The God who answers by orphanages, let him be Lord!"[3] Mrs. Hillyard, who belonged to Müller's Plymouth Brethren denomination, offered Spurgeon £20,000 if he would start an orphanage like the one he had described in *The Sword and the Trowel*, a magazine he founded in 1865. He had written that a school for the poor was needed where "all that we believe and hold dear shall be taught to the children of our poorer adherents."[4]

Spurgeon, who was born June 19, 1834, was himself a kind of

[3] Cited in Tom Nettles, *Living by Revealed Truth: The Life and Pastoral Theology of Charles Haddon Spurgeon* (Fearn, Ross-shire, Scotland: Christian Focus, 2013), 375.
[4] Cited in ibid.

orphan. His parents had not died, but they were not able to care for him at the beginning, and in his first year sent him to live with his grandparents. He recalls his exposure there to the riches of the Puritan books of his grandfather. He would be a lover of the Puritans for the rest of his life. He said he read *The Pilgrim's Progress* more than one hundred times.[5] His grandmother would give him a penny for each Isaac Watts hymn that he memorized. And his mother, after he moved back home in 1841, would read to him Puritan classics such as "Alleine's Alarm."[6]

Even before he was converted at fifteen through the preaching of a Methodist lay preacher, he knew his spiritual condition and the Puritan prescription for the remedy for his sins. He had read John Bunyan's *Grace Abounding*, Richard Baxter's *Call to the Unconverted*, and John Angell James's *The Anxious Inquirer*. But God did not open his eyes to the sweetness of the gospel until January 6, 1850, in the Primitive Methodist Church in Colchester, where he had taken refuge from a snowstorm.

Whatever his estrangement was before—from his parents and his Creator—he was now adopted into the family of God. He never looked back. With no formal theological training, he was called at the age of seventeen to be the pastor of a Congregational church in Waterbeach. Just short of two years later, at the age of nineteen, he candidated at the New Park Street Chapel, London. He started his ministry there the next year (1854). The church changed its name to the Metropolitan Tabernacle when a new building was constructed. Spurgeon would be the pastor of this congregation for thirty-eight years until his death in 1892.

The Waves of Blessing on His Preaching

Preaching was the most renowned and effective part of Spurgeon's life. He preached more than six hundred times before he was twenty.[7]

---

[5] Eric W. Hayden, "Did You Know?" in *Christian History*, Issue 29, Volume X, No. 1, 2.
[6] Joseph Alleine, *An Alarm to the Unconverted* (1671; repr., Lafayette, IN: Sovereign Grace, 2007).
[7] Hayden, "Did You Know?," 2.

After the new building opened, he was typically heard by six thousand people on the Lord's Day. He once preached to the largest indoor crowd of his life, 23,654—without electronic amplification. His sermons would eventually sell about twenty-five thousand copies a week and be translated into twenty languages.

When he came to New Park Street Chapel, there were 232 members. Thirty-eight years later, there were 5,311, with a total addition of 14,460 (an average of 380 new members a year). All of this happened even though he had no formal theological education. He was self-taught and read voraciously—about six books a week, with a phenomenal memory. At his death, his library consisted of about twelve thousand volumes. To secure the legacy of preaching for other churches and times, he founded a Pastors' College, which trained nearly nine hundred men in his lifetime.[8]

But the ever-present Lord Jesus did not spare his friend and servant the "many tribulations" Paul promised to all who would enter the kingdom of heaven (Acts 14:22). His life was hard, and by the standard of his friend Müller, short. He stood before his people for the last time on June 7, 1891, and died the following January 31 from a painful combination of rheumatism, gout, and Bright's disease. He was fifty-seven.

Neither Spurgeon's death nor his life was easy. They were not painfree. As I have walked with Spurgeon over the years, these lessons have helped me most—the lessons of living with loss and criticism and sickness and sorrow. This is what I focus on in this chapter. But first, we should see that there are other reasons why we—especially preachers—can learn so much from Spurgeon. I offer seven reasons.

1. Spurgeon Was a Preacher

We have seen already that Spurgeon's preaching, beyond question, was what gave his life such a powerful impact. The sheer quantity of his

---

[8] Ibid.

preaching is staggering. Today, his collected sermons fill sixty-three volumes, currently standing as the largest set of books by a single author in the history of Christianity.[9]

Even if his son Charles was biased, his assessment is close enough to the truth: "There was no one who could preach like my father. In inexhaustible variety, witty wisdom, vigorous proclamation, loving entreaty, and lucid teaching, with a multitude of other qualities, he must, at least in my opinion, ever be regarded as the prince of preachers."[10] Spurgeon was a preacher.

2. He Was a Truth-Driven Preacher

We should not be interested in how preachers deal with adversity if they are not first and foremost guardians and givers of unchanging biblical truth. If they find their way through adversity by other means than faithfulness to truth, they are no help to us.

Spurgeon defined the work of the preacher like this: "To know truth as it should be known, to love it as it should be loved, and then to proclaim it in the right spirit, and in its proper proportions."[11] He said to his students, "To be effective preachers you must be sound theologians."[12] He warned that "those who do away with Christian doctrine are, whether they are aware of it or not, the worst enemies of Christian living . . . [because] the coals of orthodoxy are necessary to the fire of piety."[13]

Two years before he died, he said:

Some excellent brethren seem to think more of the life than of the truth; for when I warn them that the enemy has poisoned the children's bread, they answer "Dear brother, we are sorry to hear it; and, to counteract the evil, we will open the window, and give the children fresh air." Yes, open the window, and give them fresh

---

[9] Ibid., 2.
[10] Cited in C. H. Spurgeon, *Autobiography*, vol. 2 (Edinburgh: Banner of Truth, 1973), 278.
[11] Charles Haddon Spurgeon, *An All-Round Ministry* (Edinburgh: Banner of Truth, 1960), 8.
[12] Ibid.
[13] Cited in Erroll Hulse and David Kingdon, eds., *A Marvelous Ministry: How the All-Round Ministry of Charles Haddon Spurgeon Speaks to Us Today* (Ligonier, PA: Soli Deo Gloria, 1993), 128.

air, by all means. . . . But, at the same time, this ought you to have done, and not to have left the other undone. Arrest the poison-ers, and open the windows, too. While men go on preaching false doctrine, you may talk as much as you will about deepening their spiritual life, but you will fail in it.[14]

Doctrinal truth was at the foundation of all Spurgeon's labors.

3. He Was a Bible-Believing Preacher

The truth that drove his preaching ministry was biblical truth, which he believed to be God's truth. He held up his Bible and said:

These words are God's. . . . Thou book of vast authority, thou art a proclamation from the Emperor of Heaven; far be it from me to exercise my reason in contradicting thee. . . . This is the book un-tainted by any error; but it is pure unalloyed, perfect truth. Why? Because God wrote it.[15]

There is a difference in the hearts of preachers and people where this allegiance holds sway. I once had lunch with a man who bemoaned the atmosphere of his fledgling Sunday school class. He said the class typically centered around the group's discussion. One person would raise a topic and another would find a relevant Bible verse, but after the reading of the verse, the attitude became, "Now we have heard what Jesus thinks; what do you think?" Where that atmosphere be-gins to take over the pulpit and the church, defection from truth and weakness in holiness are not far behind.

4. He Was a Soul-Winning Preacher

There was not a week that went by in Spurgeon's mature ministry that souls were not saved through his written sermons.[16] He and his elders were always on the "watch for souls" in the great congregation. "One

---

[14] Spurgeon, *An All-Round Ministry*, 374.
[15] Cited in Hulse and Kingdon, *A Marvelous Ministry*, 47.
[16] Arnold Dallimore, *Spurgeon* (Chicago: Moody Press, 1984), 198.

brother," he said, "has earned for himself the title of my hunting dog, for he is always ready to pick up the wounded birds."[17]

Spurgeon was not exaggerating when he said:

> I remember, when I have preached at different times in the country, and sometimes here, that my whole soul has agonized over men, every nerve of my body has been strained and I could have wept my very being out of my eyes and carried my whole frame away in a flood of tears, if I could but win souls.[18]

He was consumed with the glory of God and the salvation of men.

5. He Was a Calvinistic Preacher

Spurgeon was my kind of Calvinist. Let me give you a flavor of why his Calvinism drew five thousand people a week to his church rather than driving them away. He said:

> To me, Calvinism means the placing of the eternal God at the head of all things. I look at everything through its relation to God's glory. I see God first, and man far down in the list. . . . Brethren, if we live in sympathy with God, we delight to hear Him say, "I am God, and there is none else."[19]

> Puritanism, Protestantism, Calvinism [are simply] poor names which the world has given to our great and glorious faith—the doctrine of Paul the apostle, the gospel of our Lord and Savior Jesus Christ.[20]

But he did make distinctions between the full system of Calvinism, which he did embrace, and some central, evangelical doctrines shared by others that bound him together with them. For example, his favorite was the doctrine of the substitution of Christ for sinners.

---

[17] Spurgeon, *Autobiography*, vol. 2, 76.
[18] Cited in Hulse and Kingdon, *A Marvelous Ministry*, 49–50.
[19] Spurgeon, *An All-Round Ministry*, 337.
[20] Ibid., 160.

He said, "Far be it from me to imagine that Zion contains none but Calvinistic Christians within her walls, or that there are none saved who do not hold our views."[21]

He said, "I am not an outrageous Protestant generally, and I rejoice to confess that I feel sure there are some of God's people even in the Romish Church."[22] He chose a paedobaptist to be the first head of his Pastors' College, and did not make that issue a barrier to preaching in his pulpit. His communion was open to all Christians, but he said he "would rather give up his pastorate than admit any man to the church who was not obedient to his Lord's command [of baptism]."[23]

His first words in the Metropolitan Tabernacle, the place he built to preach in for thirty years, were:

> I would propose that the subject of the ministry in this house, as long as this platform shall stand and as long as this house shall be frequented by worshippers, shall be the person of Jesus Christ. I am never ashamed to avow myself a Calvinist; I do not hesitate to take the name of Baptist; but if I am asked what is my creed, I reply, "It is Jesus Christ."[24]

But Spurgeon believed that Calvinism honored Christ most fully because it was most true. And he preached it explicitly and tried to work it into the minds of his people because, he said, "Calvinism has in it a conservative force which helps to hold men to vital truth."[25]

Therefore, he was open and unashamed: "People come to me for one thing. . . . I preach to them a Calvinist creed and a Puritan morality. That is what they want and that is what they get. If they want anything else they must go elsewhere."[26]

---

[21] Cited in Hulse and Kingdon, *A Marvelous Ministry*, 65.

[22] Spurgeon, *Autobiography*, vol. 2, 21.

[23] Cited in Hulse and Kingdon, *A Marvelous Ministry*, 43.

[24] Cited in Bob L. Ross, *A Pictorial Biography of C. H. Spurgeon* (Pasadena, TX: Pilgrim Publications, 1974), 66.

[25] Cited in Hulse and Kingdon, *A Marvelous Ministry*, 121.

[26] Cited in ibid., 38.

6. He Was a Hard-Working Preacher

I do not look to soft and leisurely men to instruct me how to endure adversity. If the main answer is, "Take it easy," I look for another teacher. Take a glimpse of Spurgeon's capacity for work:

> No one living knows the toil and care I have to bear. . . . I have to look after the Orphanage, have charge of a church with four thousand members, sometimes there are marriages and burials to be undertaken, there is the weekly sermon to be revised, *The Sword and the Trowel* to be edited, and besides all that, a weekly average of five hundred letters to be answered. This, however, is only half my duty, for there are innumerable churches established by friends, with the affairs of which I am closely connected, to say nothing of the cases of difficulty which are constantly being referred to me.[27]

At his fiftieth birthday, a list was read of sixty-six organizations that he had founded and conducted. The Earl of Shaftesbury, a distinguished English peer, was there and said, "This list of associations, instituted by his genius, and superintended by his care, were more than enough to occupy the minds and hearts of fifty ordinary men."[28]

He typically read six substantial books a week and could remember what he read and where to find it.[29] He produced more than 140 books of his own—such as *The Treasury of David*, which was twenty years in the making, and *Morning and Evening* and *Commenting on Commentaries* and *John Ploughman's Talk* and *Our Own Hymnbook*.[30]

He often worked eighteen hours in a day. The missionary David Livingstone asked him once, "How do you manage to do two men's work in a single day?" Spurgeon replied, "You have forgotten there are two of us."[31] I think he meant the presence of Christ's energizing power that we read about in Colossians 1:29, where Paul says, "I toil, struggling with all his energy that he powerfully works within me."

---

[27] Spurgeon, *Autobiography*, vol. 2, 192.
[28] Cited in Dallimore, *Spurgeon*, 173.
[29] Hayden, "Did You Know?," 2.
[30] Dallimore, *Spurgeon*, 195.
[31] Hayden, "Did You Know?," 3.

Spurgeon's attitude toward sacrificial labor would not be acceptable today, when the primacy of "wellness" seems to hold sway. He said:

> If by excessive labour, we die before reaching the average age of man, worn out in the Master's service, then glory be to God, we shall have so much less of earth and so much more of Heaven![32]

> It is our duty and our privilege to exhaust our lives for Jesus. We are not to be living specimens of men in fine preservation, but living sacrifices, whose lot is to be consumed.[33]

Behind this radical viewpoint were some deep biblical convictions that came through the apostle Paul's teaching. One of these convictions Spurgeon expressed like this: "We can only produce life in others by the wear and tear of our own being. This is a natural and spiritual law—that fruit can only come to the seed by its spending and be spent even to self-exhaustion."[34]

The apostle Paul said, "If we are afflicted, it is for your comfort and salvation" (2 Cor. 1:6) and "Death is at work in us, but life in you" (4:12). And he said that his own sufferings were the completion of Christ's sufferings for the sake of the church (Col. 1:24).

Another biblical conviction behind Spurgeon's radical view of pastoral zeal is expressed like this:

> Satisfaction with results will be the [death] knell of progress. No man is good who thinks that he cannot be better. He has no holiness who thinks that he is holy enough.[35]

In other words, he was driven with a passion never to be satisfied with the measure of his holiness or the extent of his service (see Phil. 3:12). The year he turned forty, he delivered a message to his pastors' conference with the one-word title "Forward!"[36] In it, he said:

---

[32] Spurgeon, *An All-Round Ministry*, 126–27.
[33] Spurgeon, *Lectures to My Students*, 157.
[34] Spurgeon, *An All-Round Ministry*, 177.
[35] Ibid., 352.
[36] Ibid., 32–58.

In every minister's life there should be traces of stern labour.
Brethren, do something; do something; *do something*. While Com-
mittees waste their time over resolutions, do something. While
Societies and Unions are making constitutions, let us win souls.
Too often we discuss, and discuss, and discuss, while Satan only
laughs in his sleeve. . . . Get to work and quit yourselves like men.[37]

I think the word *indefatigable* was created for people like Spurgeon.

7. He Was a Maligned and Suffering Preacher

He knew the whole range of adversity that most preachers suffer—
and a lot more.

*Spurgeon knew the everyday, homegrown variety of frustration and disap-
pointment from lukewarm members.*

[Pastors] understand what one cold-hearted man can do if he gets
at you on Sunday morning with the information that Mrs. Smith
and all her family are offended, and therefore, their pew is vacant.
You did not want to know of that Lady's protest just before entering the pulpit, and it does not help you.[38]

Or perhaps, even worse, it can happen after the service:

What terrible blankets some professors are! Their remarks after a
sermon are enough to stagger you. . . . You have been pleading as
for life or death and they have been calculating how many seconds
the sermon occupied, and grudging you the odd five minutes beyond the usual hour.[39]

It's even worse, he says, if the calculating observer is one of your dea-
cons: "Thou shalt not yoke the ox and the ass together was a merciful
precept: but when a laborious, ox-like minister comes to be yoked to
a deacon who is not another ox, it becomes hard work to plough."[40]

---

[37] Ibid., 55.
[38] Ibid., 358.
[39] Spurgeon, *Lectures to My Students*, 310.
[40] Ibid., 311.

He also knew the extraordinary calamities that befall us once in a lifetime.

On October 19, 1856, he preached for the first time in the Music Hall of the Royal Surrey Gardens because his own church would not hold the people. The seating capacity of ten thousand was far exceeded as the crowds pressed in. Someone shouted, "Fire!" and there was great panic in parts of the building. Seven people were killed in the stampede and scores were injured.

Spurgeon was twenty-two years old and was overcome by this calamity. He said later, "Perhaps never soul went so near the burning furnace of insanity, and yet came away unharmed."[41] But not all agreed he was unharmed. The specter brooded over him for years, and one close friend and biographer said, "I cannot but think, from what I saw, that his comparatively early death might be in some measure due to the furnace of mental suffering he endured on and after that fearful night."[42]

Spurgeon also knew the adversity of family pain.

He had married Susannah on January 8 of the same year of the calamity at Surrey Gardens. His only two children, twin sons, were born the day after the calamity, on October 20. Susannah was never able to have more children. In 1865 (nine years later), when she was thirty-three years old, she became a virtual invalid and seldom heard her husband preach for the next twenty-seven years until his death. Some kind of rare cervical operations were attempted in 1869 by James Simpson, the father of modern gynecology, but to no avail.[43] So to Spurgeon's other burdens were added the care of a sickly wife and the inability to have more children, though his own mother had given birth to seventeen.

Spurgeon knew unbelievable physical suffering.

He suffered from gout, rheumatism, and Bright's disease (inflam-

---

[41] Cited in *Great Preaching on the Deity of Christ*, comp. Curtis Hutson (Murfreesboro, TN: Sword of the Lord, 2000), 206.
[42] Cited in Darrel W. Amundsen, "The Anguish and Agonies of Charles Spurgeon," in *Christian History*, Issue 29, Vol. X, No. 1, 23.
[43] Hulse and Kingdon, *A Marvelous Ministry*, 38–39.

mation of the kidneys). His first attack of gout came in 1869, at the age of thirty-five. It became progressively worse, so that "approximately one third of the last twenty-two years of his ministry was spent out of the Tabernacle pulpit, either suffering, or convalescing, or taking precautions against the return of illness."[44] In a letter to a friend, he wrote, "Lucian says, 'I thought a cobra had bitten me, and filled my veins with poison; but it was worse—it was gout.' That was written from experience, I know."[45]

So for more than half of his ministry, Spurgeon dealt with ever-increasing recurrent pain in his joints that cut him down from the pulpit and from his labors again and again. The diseases eventually took his life at age fifty-seven, when he was convalescing in Mentone, France.

In addition to the physical suffering, Spurgeon had to endure a lifetime of public ridicule and slander, sometimes of the most vicious kind.

In April 1855, the *Essex Standard* carried an article with these words:

> His style is that of the vulgar colloquial, varied by rant. . . . All the most solemn mysteries of our holy religion are by him rudely, roughly, and impiously handled. Common sense is outraged and decency disgusted. His rantings are interspersed with coarse anecdotes.[46]

The *Sheffield and Rotherham Independent* said:

> He is a nine days' wonder—a comet that has suddenly shot across the religious atmosphere. He has gone up like a rocket and ere long will come down like a stick.[47]

His wife kept a bulging scrapbook of such criticisms from the years 1855–1856. Some of it was easy to brush off. Most of it wasn't. In 1857, he wrote, "Down on my knees have I often fallen, with the hot sweat

---

[44] Iain H. Murray, ed., *Letters of Charles Haddon Spurgeon* (Edinburgh: Banner of Truth, 1992), 166n1.
[45] Cited in ibid., 165.
[46] Cited in Hulse and Kingdon, *A Marvelous Ministry*, 35.
[47] Cited in ibid.

rising from my brow under some fresh slander poured upon me; in an agony of grief my heart has been well-nigh broken."[48]

His fellow ministers from the right and left criticized him. From the left, Joseph Parker wrote:

> Mr. Spurgeon was absolutely destitute of intellectual benevolence. If men saw as he did they were orthodox; if they saw things in some other way they were heterodox, pestilent and unfit to lead the minds of students or inquirers. Mr. Spurgeon's was a superlative egotism; not the shilly-shallying, timid, half-disguised egotism that cuts off its own head, but the full-grown, over-powering, sublime egotism that takes the chief seat as if by right. The only colors which Mr. Spurgeon recognized were black and white.[49]

And from the right, James Wells, the hyper-Calvinist, wrote, "I have—most solemnly have—my doubts as to the Divine reality of his conversion."[50]

All the embattlements of his life came to a climax in the Downgrade Controversy, as Spurgeon fought unsuccessfully for the doctrinal integrity of the Baptist Union. In October 1887, he withdrew from the Union. And the following January, he was officially and publicly censured by a vote of the Union for his manner of protest.[51]

Eight years earlier, he had said: "Men cannot say anything worse of me than they have said. I have been belied from head to foot, and misrepresented to the last degree. My good looks are gone, and none can damage me much now."[52]

He gives an example of the kinds of distortions and misrepresentations that were typical in the Downgrade Controversy:

> The doctrine of eternal punishment has been scarcely raised by me in this controversy; but the "modern thought" advocates continue

---

[48] Cited in Amundsen, "The Anguish and Agonies of Charles Spurgeon," 23.
[49] Cited in Hulse and Kingdon, *A Marvelous Ministry*, 69.
[50] Cited in ibid., 35.
[51] Ibid., 126.
[52] Cited in ibid., 159.

to hold it up on all occasions, all the while turning the wrong side of it outwards.[53]

But even though he usually sounded rough and ready, the pain was overwhelming and deadly. In May 1891, eight months before he died, he said to a friend: "Good-bye; you will never see me again. This fight is killing me."[54]

Spurgeon had recurrent battles with depression.

This final adversity was the result of the others. It is not easy to imagine the omnicompetent, eloquent, brilliant, full-of-energy Spurgeon weeping like a baby for no reason that he could think of. In 1858, at age twenty-four, it happened for the first time. He said, "My spirits were sunken so low that I could weep by the hour like a child, and yet I knew not what I wept for."[55] He added:

Causeless depression cannot be reasoned with, nor can David's harp charm it away by sweet discoursings. As well fight with the mist as with this shapeless, undefinable, yet all-beclouding hopelessness. . . . The iron bolt which so mysteriously fastens the door of hope and holds our spirits in gloomy prison, needs a heavenly hand to push it back.[56]

He saw his depression as his "worst feature." "Despondency," he said, "is not a virtue; I believe it is a vice. I am heartily ashamed of myself for falling into it, but I am sure there is no remedy for it like a holy faith in God."[57]

In spite of all these sufferings and persecutions, Spurgeon endured to the end, and was able to preach mightily until his last sermon at the Tabernacle on June 7, 1891. The question I have asked in reading this man's life and work is, *how did he preserve and preach through this adversity?*

---

[53] Cited in ibid., 288.
[54] Cited in Amundsen, "The Anguish and Agonies of Charles Spurgeon," 25.
[55] Cited in ibid., 24.
[56] Spurgeon, *Lectures to My Students*, 163.
[57] Cited in Amundsen, "The Anguish and Agonies of Charles Spurgeon," 24.

PREACHING THROUGH ADVERSITY

There were innumerable strategies of grace in the life of Charles Spurgeon. The ones I have chosen to mention are limited, and I chose them mainly because they have impacted me personally, but the scope of this man's strategies and the wisdom of his warfare were immense.

1. Spurgeon saw his depression as the design of God for the good of his ministry and the glory of Christ.

I begin with the issue of despondency and depression because if this one can be conquered, all the other forms of adversity that feed into it will be nullified. What comes through again and again in Spurgeon's writings is his unwavering belief in the sovereignty of God in all his afflictions. More than anything else, it seems, this kept him from caving in to the adversities of his life. He writes:

> It would be a very sharp and trying experience to me to think that I have an affliction which God never sent me, that the bitter cup was never filled by his hand, that my trials were never measured out by him, nor sent to me by his arrangement of their weight and quantity.[58]

This is exactly the opposite strategy of modern thought, even much evangelical thought, which recoils from the implications of God's infinity. If God is God, he not only knows what is coming, but he knows it *because* he designed it (Isa. 46:10; Jer. 1:12). For Spurgeon, this view of God was not an argument for debate; it was a means of survival. Our afflictions are the health regimen of an infinitely wise Physician. Spurgeon told his students:

> I dare say the greatest earthly blessing that God can give to any of us is health, with the exception of sickness. . . . If some men that I know of could only be favoured with a month of rheumatism, it would, by God's grace mellow them marvelously.[59]

---

[58] Cited in ibid., 25.
[59] Spurgeon, *An All-Round Ministry*, 384.

He meant this mainly for himself. Though he dreaded suffering and would avoid it, he said:

> I am afraid that all the grace that I have got of my comfortable and easy times and happy hours, might almost lie on a penny. But the good that I have received from my sorrows, and pains, and griefs, is altogether incalculable. . . . Affliction is the best bit of furniture in my house. It is the best book in a minister's library.[60]

He saw three specific purposes of God in his struggle with depression. The first is that it functioned like the apostle Paul's thorn to keep him humble, lest he be lifted up in himself. Spurgeon said the Lord's work is summed up in these words:

> "Not by might nor by power but by my Spirit, saith the Lord." Instruments shall be used, but their intrinsic weakness shall be clearly manifested; there shall be no division of the glory, no diminishing of the honor due to the Great Worker. . . . Those who are honoured of their Lord in public have usually to endure a secret chastening, or to carry a peculiar cross, lest by any means they exalt themselves, and fall into the snare of the devil.[61]

The second purpose of God in his despondency was the unexpected power it gave to his ministry:

> One Sabbath morning, I preached from the text, "My God, My God, why has Thou forsaken Me?" and though I did not say so, yet I preached my own experience. I heard my own chains clank while I tried to preach to my fellow-prisoners in the dark; but I could not tell why I was brought into such an awful horror of darkness, for which I condemned myself. On the following Monday evening, a man came to see me who bore all the marks of despair upon his countenance. His hair seemed to stand up right, and his eyes were ready to start from their sockets. He said to me, after a little

---

[60] Cited in Amundsen, "The Anguish and Agonies of Charles Spurgeon," 25.
[61] Cited in ibid., 163–64.

parleying, "I never before, in my life, heard any man speak who seemed to know my heart. Mine is a terrible case; but on Sunday morning you painted me to the life, and preached as if you had been inside my soul." By God's grace I saved that man from suicide, and led him into gospel light and liberty; but I know I could not have done it if I had not myself been confined in the dungeon in which he lay. I tell you the story, brethren, because you sometimes may not understand your own experience, and the perfect people may condemn you for having it; but what know they of God's servants? You and I have to suffer much for the sake of the people of our charge. . . . You may be in Egyptian darkness, and you may wonder why such a horror chills your marrow; but you may be altogether in the pursuit of your calling, and be led of the Spirit to a position of sympathy with desponding minds.[62]

The third design of his depression was what he called a prophetic signal for the future:

This depression comes over me whenever the Lord is preparing a larger blessing for my ministry; the cloud is black before it breaks, and overshadows before it yields its deluge of mercy. Depression has now become to me as a prophet in rough clothing, a John the Baptist, heralding the nearer coming of my Lord's richer benison.[63]

I would say with Spurgeon that in the darkest hours, it is the sovereign goodness of God that has given me the strength to go on—the granite promise that he rules over my circumstances and means it for good, no matter what anyone else means.

2. Spurgeon supplemented his theological survival strategy with God's natural means of survival—his use of rest and nature.

For all his talk about spending and being spent, he counsels us to rest and take a day off and open ourselves to the healing powers God has put in the world of nature.

---

[62] Spurgeon, *An All-Round Ministry*, 221–22.
[63] Spurgeon, *Lectures to My Students*, 160.

"Our Sabbath is our day of toil," he said, "and if we do not rest upon some other day we shall break down."[64] Eric Hayden reminds us that Spurgeon "kept, when possible, Wednesday as his day of rest."[65] More than that, Spurgeon said to his students:

> It is wisdom to take occasional furlough. In the long run, we shall do more by sometimes doing less. On, on, on forever, without recreation may suit spirits emancipated from this "heavy clay," but while we are in this tabernacle, we must every now and then cry halt, and serve the Lord by holy inaction and consecrated leisure. Let no tender conscience doubt the lawfulness of going out of harness for a while.[66]

In my pastoral ministry experience, I can testify that time off is crucial for breathing a different spiritual air. When we take time away from the press of duty, Spurgeon recommends that we breathe country air and let the beauty of nature do its appointed work. He confesses that "sedentary habits have tendency to create despondency . . . especially in the months of fog." He then counsels, "A mouthful of sea air, or a stiff walk in the wind's face would not give grace to the soul, but it would yield oxygen to the body, which is next best."[67]

At this point, let me add a personal word to you who are younger. In my years of pastoral ministry, I noticed significant changes in my body and soul. They were partly owing to changing circumstances, but much was owing to a changing constitution. First, I had to reduce my calorie intake to keep from gaining unhelpful weight. During the course of my ministry and aging, my metabolism stopped functioning the way it once did. Second, I grew to become emotionally less resilient when I didn't get adequate sleep. There were early days when I would work without regard to sleep, and afterward I would feel energized and motivated. However, as I entered my forties, adequate

---

[64] Ibid., 160.
[65] Eric W. Hayden, *Highlights in the Life of C. H. Spurgeon* (Pasadena, TX: Pilgrim Publications, 1990), 103.
[66] Spurgeon, *Lectures to My Students*, 161.
[67] Ibid., 158.

sleep was no longer a matter of staying healthy, but a matter of staying in the ministry. It is irrational that my future should look bleaker when I get four or five hours of sleep for several nights in a row, but that point is irrelevant. The fact is that my future *felt* bleaker, and I must live within the limits of that fact. I commend sufficient sleep to you, for the sake of your proper assessment of God and his promises.

Spurgeon was right when he said:

> The condition of your body must be attended to. . . . A little more
> . . . common sense would be a great gain to some who are ultra
> spiritual, and attribute all their moods of feeling to some super-
> natural cause when the real reason lies far nearer to hand. Has it
> not often happened that dyspepsia has been mistaken for backslid-
> ing, and bad digestion has been set down as a hard heart?[68]

3. Spurgeon consistently nourished his soul by communion with Christ through prayer and meditation.

It was a great mercy to me at an embattled point in my ministry that I discovered John Owen's book *Communion with God*. It nourished me again and again as my soul asked, "Can God spread a table in the wilderness?"

Spurgeon warned his students:

> Never neglect your spiritual meals, or you will lack stamina and
> your spirits will sink. Live on the substantial doctrines of grace,
> and you will outlive and out-work those who delight in the pastry
> and syllabubs of "modern thought."[69]

I think one of the reasons Spurgeon was so rich in language and full in doctrinal substance and strong in the spirit, in spite of his despondency and his physical oppression and his embattlements, is that he was always immersed in a great book—six books a week. Most of us cannot match that number, but we can always be walking with

68 Ibid., 312.
69 Ibid., 310.

some great "see-er" of God. Over the years, I've learned that the key in all good reading of theology is to strive in the reading for utterly real fellowship with Christ. Spurgeon said:

> Above all, feed the flame with intimate fellowship with Christ. No man was ever cold in heart who lived with Jesus on such terms as John and Mary did of old. . . . I never met with a half-hearted preacher who was much in communion with the Lord Jesus.[70]

In many ways, Spurgeon was a child in his communion with God. He did not speak in complex terms about anything too strange or mystical. In fact, as we noted in the introduction, his prayer life seems to have been more businesslike than contemplative:

> When I pray, I like to go to God just as I go to a bank clerk when I have [a] cheque to be cashed. I walk in, put the cheque down on the counter, and the clerk gives me my money, I take it up, and go about my business. I do not know that I ever stopped in a bank five minutes to talk with the clerks; when I have received my change I go away and attend to other matters. That is how I like to pray; but there is a way of praying that seems like lounging near the mercy seat as though one had no particular reason for being found there.[71]

This may not be entirely exemplary. It may dishonor the Lord to treat him like a bank clerk rather than like a mountain spring. But we would make a mistake if we thought that Spurgeon's businesslike praying was anything other than childlike communion with his Father.

The most touching description I have read of his communion with God comes from 1871, when he was in terrible pain with gout:

> When I was racked some months ago with pain, to an extreme degree, so that I could no longer bear it without crying out, I asked all to go from the room, and leave me alone; and then I had nothing I could say to God but this, "Thou are my Father, and I am thy

---

[70] Ibid., 315.
[71] Cited in Hulse and Kingdon, *A Marvelous Ministry*, 46–47.

child; and thou, as a Father art tender and full of mercy. I could not bear to see my child suffer as thou makest me suffer, and if I saw him tormented as I am now, I would do what I could to help him, and put my arms under him to sustain him. Wilt thou hide thy face from me, my Father? Wilt thou still lay on a heavy hand, and not give me a smile from thy countenance?" . . . So I pleaded, and I ventured to say, when I was quiet, and they came back who watched me: "I shall never have such pain again from this moment, for God has heard my prayer." I bless God that ease came and the racking pain never returned.[72]

If we are going to preach through adversity, we have to live in communion with God on such intimate terms—speaking to him our needs and our pain, and feeding on the grace of his promises and the revelations of his glory.

4. Spurgeon rekindled his zeal and passion to preach by fixing his eyes on eternity rather than on the immediate price of faithfulness.

The apostle Paul saw that the outer nature was wasting away. What kept him going was the abiding assurance that his momentary affliction was working for him an eternal weight of glory. And so he looked to the things that are eternal (2 Cor. 4:16–18). So did Spurgeon:

O brethren, we shall soon have to die! We look each other in the face to-day in health, but there will come a day when others will look down upon our pallid countenances as we lie in our coffins. . . . It will matter little to us who shall gaze upon us then, but it will matter eternally how we have discharged our work during our lifetime.[73]

When our hearts grow faint and our zeal wavers for the task of preaching, Spurgeon calls us to:

Meditate with deep solemnity upon the fate of the lost sinner. . . . Shun all views of future punishment which would make it appear

---

[72] Cited in Amundsen, "The Anguish and Agonies of Charles Spurgeon," 24.
[73] Spurgeon, *An All-Round Ministry*, 76.

less terrible, and so take off the edge of your anxiety to save im-
mortals from the quenchless flame. . . . Think much also of the
bliss of the sinner saved, and like holy Baxter derive rich argu-
ments from "the saints' everlasting rest." . . . There will be no fear
of your being lethargic if you are continually familiar with eternal
realities.[74]

Short of eternity, he took the long view when it came to his own
persecution. In the Downgrade Controversy, Spurgeon said:

Posterity must be considered. I do not look so much at what is to
happen to-day, for these things relate to eternity. For my part, I am
quite willing to be eaten of dogs for the next fifty years; but the
more distant future shall vindicate me. I have dealt honestly before
the living God. My brother, do the same.[75]

To keep on preaching in storms of adversity, you must look well
beyond the crisis and feelings of the hour. You must look to what
history will make of your faithfulness, and most of all, what God will
make of it at the last day.

5. Spurgeon had settled who he was and would not be paralyzed
by external criticism or internal second-guessing.

One of the great perils of living under continual criticism is that
it is a constant call for you to be other than what you are. This is
especially problematic because a humble saint always wants to be a
better person than he is.

Tim Stafford, a freelance writer and senior writer for *Christianity Today*, warns us against taking Spurgeon's counsel in the wrong
way—a way that short-circuits the process of sanctification. He tells
his story by way of illustration:

I was shy, and often shy people retreat into themselves, unknow-
ingly giving the impression of unfriendly aloofness. In college, I
began to realize that other people's image of me did not match my

---

[74] Spurgeon, *Lectures to My Students*, 315.
[75] Spurgeon, *An All-Round Ministry*, 360–61.

image of myself. Those who did not know me well saw me as stern, aloof, and judgmental. Nobody told me so directly. Once I began to catch on, however, I was hit by the message from all sides.

This pained me deeply, because it was not true. I knew what was inside me. I was as aloof as a puppy dog. I was soft-hearted, if anything. I cared about people. I craved friendship.

I began to try to rewrite my life. I began consciously to say nice things to people, to let them know that I appreciated and liked them. I tried to act warmly. I began to hold my tongue when I had something to say that might be construed as critical or snobbish.

And I hated it. It felt horribly unnatural. I despised having to watch my words, having to mull over every interaction to see whether I had handled it well and gotten my message across. Why couldn't I just be myself? I was, I suppose, a true child of the sixties: I believed that acting sincerely was enough. Now I felt that I was acting insincerely, putting on an act.

My changes did bring noticeably better results, though. People told me I was different. They told me I seemed warmer, happier. People opened up to me. People sought me out. I liked those differences. And I found that I got used to the act I was putting on. Over months and years it grew comfortable. Eventually, it became liberating. It became me.[76]

That is a good and wise caution against using "Be yourself" as an excuse to never change more fully into the likeness of Christ. The New Testament everywhere presumes that change is possible through Christ and is to be pursued—"from one degree of glory to another" (2 Cor. 3:18).

But Spurgeon knew this as well as we do. When he spoke of change, he was talking about something different. He was pointing out that in the clash of tongues, when your adversaries are saying that you cast out demons by the prince of demons, you'd better know if that is true or not. If you doubt yourself because of such criticism,

---

[76] Tim Stafford, "Can We Talk?" in *Christianity Today*, Oct. 2, 1995.

you will not survive in the ministry. There is a great danger here of losing your bearings in a sea of self-doubt and not knowing who you are—not being able to say with Paul, "By the grace of God I am what I am" (1 Cor. 15:10). Spurgeon felt this danger keenly.

In comparing one ministerial identity with another, he reminded other pastors that at Jesus's Last Supper, there was a chalice for drinking the wine and there was a basin for washing feet. Then he said:

> I protest that I have no choice whether to be the chalice or the basin. Fain would I be whichever the Lord wills so long as he will but use me. . . . So you, my brother, you may be the cup, and I will be the basin; but let the cup be a cup, and the basin a basin, and each one of us just what he is fitted to be. Be yourself, dear brother, for, if you are not yourself, you cannot be anybody else; and so, you see, you must be nobody. . . . Do not be a mere copyist, a borrower, a spoiler of other men's notes. Say what God has said to you, and say it in your own way; and when it is so said, plead personally for the Lord's blessing upon it.[77]

I would also add, plead to the Lord personally that his purifying blood be upon it, too, because none of our best labors is untainted. The danger, though, is to let the truth paralyze you with fear of man and doubt of self.

Eleven years later, in 1886, Spurgeon struck the same anvil again:

> Friend, be true to your own destiny! One man would make a splendid preacher of downright hard-hitting Saxon; why must he ruin himself by cultivating an ornate style? . . . Apollos has the gift of eloquence; why must he copy blunt Cephas? Every man in his own order.[78]

Spurgeon illustrates with his own struggle to be responsive to criticism during the Downgrade Controversy. For a season, he tried to

---

[77] Spurgeon, *An All-Round Ministry*, 73–74.
[78] Ibid., 232–33.

adapt his language to the critics. But there came a time when he had to be what he was.

> I have found it utterly impossible to please, let me say or do what I will. One becomes somewhat indifferent when dealing with those whom every word offends. I notice that, when I have measured my words, and weight my sentences most carefully, I have then offended most; while some of my stronger utterances have passed unnoticed. Therefore, I am comparatively careless as to how my expressions may be received, and only anxious that they may be in themselves just and true.[79]

If you are to survive and go on preaching in an atmosphere of controversy, there comes a point where you have done your best to weigh the claims of your critics and take them to heart, and must now say, "By the grace of God I am what I am." We must bring an end to the deranging second-guessing that threatens to destroy the very soul.

6. *Spurgeon found the strength to go on preaching in the midst of adversity and setbacks from the assured sovereign triumph of Christ.*

This, we saw in the introduction, is what bound him together with George Müller and Hudson Taylor in the great camaraderie of confidence in the goodness, glory, and power of God. Near the end of his life, around 1890, in his last address at his pastors' conference, Spurgeon compared adversity and the ebb of truth to the ebbing tide:

> You never met an old salt, down by the sea, who was in trouble because the tide had been ebbing out for hours. No! He waits confidently for the turn of the tide, and it comes in due time. Yonder rock has been uncovered during the last half-hour, and if the sea continues to ebb out for weeks, there will be no water in the English Channel, and the French will walk over from Cherbourg. Nobody talks in that childish way, for such an ebb will never come. Nor will we speak as though the gospel would be routed, and eternal truth driven out of the land. We serve an almighty Master. . . .

---

[79] Ibid., 282–83.

If our Lord does but stamp his foot, he can win for himself all the nations of the earth against heathenism, and Mohammedanism, and Agnosticism, and Modern-thought, and every other foul error. Who is he that can harm us if we follow Jesus? How can his cause be defeated? At his will, converts will flock to his truth as numerous as the sands of the sea. . . . Wherefore be of good courage, and go on your way singing [and preaching!]:

> The winds of hell have blown
> The world its hate hath shown,
> Yet it is not o'erthrown.
> Hallelujah for the Cross!
> It shall never suffer loss!
> The Lord of hosts is with us,
> the God of Jacob is our refuge.[80]

---

[80] Ibid., 395–96.

If it is really good for me, my darling wife will be raised up again; sick as she is. God will restore her again. But if she is not restored again, then it would not be a good thing for me. And so my heart was at rest. I was satisfied with God. And all this springs, as I have often said before, from taking God at His word, believing what He says.

George Müller

2

George Müller

A Strategy for Showing God—Simple Faith,
Sacred Scripture, Satisfaction in God

An Immigrant with Large Vision

George Müller was a native German (a Prussian). He was born in Kroppenstaedt on September 27, 1805, and lived almost the entire nineteenth century. He died March 10, 1898, at the age of ninety-two. He saw the great Awakening of 1859, which, he said, "led to the conversion of hundreds of thousands."[1] He did follow-up work for D. L. Moody,[2] preached for Charles Spurgeon,[3] and inspired the missionary faith of Hudson Taylor.[4]

He spent most of his life in Bristol, England, and pastored the same church there for over sixty-six years—a kind of independent, premillennial,[5] Calvinistic[6] Baptist[7] church that celebrated the Lord's supper weekly[8] and admitted non-baptized people into membership.[9]

---

[1] George Müller, *A Narrative of Some of the Lord's Dealings with George Müller, Written by Himself, Jehovah Magnified. Addresses by George Müller Complete and Unabridged*, 2 vols. (Muskegon, MI: Dust and Ashes, 2003), 1:646.
[2] Ibid., 2:675.
[3] Arthur T. Pierson, *George Müller of Bristol: His Life of Prayer and Faith* (Grand Rapids, MI: Kregel, 1999), 248. Originally published as "Authorized Memoir" (Old Tappan, NJ: Revell, 1899).
[4] Ibid., 354.
[5] Müller, *A Narrative*, 1:41.
[6] Ibid., 1:39–40.
[7] Ibid., 1:53.
[8] Ibid., 1:191
[9] Ibid., 1:140.

If this sounds unconventional, that would be accurate. He was a maverick not only in his church life, but in almost all the areas of his life. But his eccentricities were almost all large-hearted and directed outward for the good of others. A. T. Pierson, who wrote the biography that Müller's son-in-law endorsed as authoritative,[10] captured the focus of this big-hearted eccentricity when he said that Müller "devised large and liberal things for the Lord's cause."[11]

A New and Different Institution

In 1834 (when he was twenty-eight), Müller founded the Scripture Knowledge Institution for Home and Abroad[12] because he was disillusioned with the postmillennialism, the liberalism, and the worldly strategies (such as going into debt[13]) of existing mission organizations.[14] This Institution eventually developed five branches that oversaw: (1) schools for children and adults to teach Bible knowledge, (2) Bible distribution, (3) book and tract distribution, (4) missionary support, and (5) "to board, clothe and Scripturally educate *destitute* children who have lost BOTH parents by death."[15]

The accomplishments of all five branches were significant. In Müller's own words, here is a summary of accomplishments up to May 1868:

> Above Sixteen Thousand Five Hundred children or grown up persons were taught in the various Schools, entirely supported by the Institution; more than Forty-Four Thousand and Five Hundred Copies of the Bible, and above Forty Thousand and Six Hundred New Testaments, and above Twenty Thousand other smaller portions of

---

[10] Pierson, *George Müller*, 13.
[11] Ibid., 264.
[12] Müller, *A Narrative*, 1:80.
[13] "Are you in debt? Then make confession of sin respecting it. Sincerely confess to the Lord that you have sinned against Rom. xiii. 8. And if you are resolved no more to contract debt, whatever may be the result, and you are waiting on the Lord, and truly trust in Him, your present debts will soon be paid. Are you out of debt? then whatever your future want may be, be resolved, in the strength of Jesus, rather to suffer the greatest privation, whilst waiting upon God for help, than to use unscriptural means, such as borrowing, taking goods on credit, etc., to deliver yourselves. This way needs but to be tried, in order that its excellency may be enjoyed." Ibid., 1:251.
[14] Ibid., 1:80–81.
[15] Ibid., 2:365–375. The italics and capital letters are Müller's.

the Holy Scriptures, in various languages, were circulated from the formation of the Institution up to May 26, 1868; and about Thirty-one Millions of Tracts and Books, likewise in several languages, were circulated. There were, likewise, from the commencement, Missionaries assisted by the funds of the Institution, and of late years more than One Hundred and Twenty in number. On this Object alone Seventy six Thousand One Hundred and Thirty-seven Pounds were expended from the beginning, up to May 26, 1868. Also 2,412 Orphans were under our care, and five large houses, at an expense of above One Hundred and Ten Thousand Pounds were erected, for the accommodation of 2,050 Orphans. With regard to the spiritual results, eternity alone can unfold them; yet even in so far as we have already seen fruit, we have abundant *cause for* praise and thanksgiving.[16]

A LOVER OF ORPHANS

But of all these accomplishments of the Institution, the one Müller was known for around the world—in his own lifetime, and still today—was the orphan ministry. He built five large orphan houses and cared for 10,024 orphans in his lifetime. When he started in 1834, there were accommodations for thirty-six hundred orphans in all of England, and twice that many children under eight were in prison.[17] One of the great effects of Müller's ministry was to inspire others so that "fifty years after Mr. Müller began his work, at least one hundred thousand orphans were cared for in England alone."[18]

He prayed in millions of dollars (in today's currency) for the orphans, and never asked anyone directly for money. He never took a salary in the last sixty-eight years of his ministry, but trusted God to put in people's hearts to send him what he needed. He never took out a loan or went into debt.[19] And neither he nor the orphans were ever hungry.

---

[16] Ibid., 2:314. The italics are Müller's.
[17] Pierson, *George Müller*, 274.
[18] Ibid.
[19] "In looking back upon the Thirty One years, during which this Institution had been in operation, I had, as will be seen, by the Grace of God, kept to the original principles, on which, for His honour, it was established on March 5, 1834. For 1, during the whole of this time I had avoided going in debt; and never had a period been brought to a close, but I had some money in hand. Great as my trials

A DREAM OF MISSIONS COME TRUE

He did all this while he was preaching three times a week from 1830 to 1898, at least ten thousand times.[20] And when he turned seventy, he fulfilled a lifelong dream of missionary work for the next seventeen years, until he was eighty-seven. He traveled to forty-two countries,[21] preaching an average of once a day[22] and addressing some three million people.[23] He preached nine times in my hometown of Minneapolis in 1880 (nine years after the founding of Bethlehem Baptist Church, where I served as pastor).

From the end of his travels in 1892 (when he was eighty-seven) until his death in March 1898, he preached in his church and worked for the Scripture Knowledge Institution. At age ninety-two, not long before he died, he wrote, "I have been able, every day and all the day, to work, and that with ease, as seventy years since."[24] He led a prayer meeting at his church on the evening of Wednesday, March 9, 1898. The next day, a cup of tea was taken to him at seven in the morning, but no answer came to the knock on the door. He was found dead on the floor beside his bed.[25]

The funeral was held the following Monday in Bristol, where he had served for sixty-six years. "Tens of thousands of people reverently stood along the route of the simple procession; men left their workshops and offices, women left their elegant homes or humble kitchens, all seeking to pay a last token of respect."[26] A thousand children gathered for a service at the Orphan House No. 3. They had now "for a second time lost a 'father.'"[27]

---

of faith might have been, I never contracted debt; for I judged, that, if God's time was come for any enlargement, He would also give the means, and that, until He supplied them, I had quietly to wait His time, and not to act before His time was fully come." Müller, *A Narrative*, 2:291. On his view of debt, see also 1:25, 62, 83, 169, 172, 213, 251, 259, 316–17, 403.

[20] Pierson, *George Müller*, 305.

[21] George Müller, *Autobiography of George Müller, or A Million and a Half in Answer to Prayer*, comp. G. Fred Bergin (Denton, TX: Westminster Literature Resources, 2003), ix.

[22] Pierson, *George Müller*, 305.

[23] Ibid., 257.

[24] Cited in ibid., 283.

[25] Ibid., 285.

[26] Ibid., 285–86.

[27] Ibid., 286.

PRECIOUS WIVES

Müller had been married twice: to Mary Groves when he was twenty-five and to Susannah Sangar when he was sixty-six. Mary bore him four children. Two were stillborn. One son, Elijah, died when he was a year old. Müller's daughter Lydia married James Wright, who succeeded him as the head of the Institution. But she died in 1890 at fifty-seven years of age. Five years later, Müller lost his second wife, just three years before he died. And so he outlived his family and was left alone with his Savior, his church, and two thousand children. He had been married to Mary for thirty-nine years and to Susannah for twenty-three years. He preached Mary's funeral sermon when he was sixty-four[28] and preached Susannah's funeral sermon when he was ninety.[29] It's what he said in the face of this loss and pain that gives us the key to his life.

MARY'S DEATH AND THE KEY TO HIS LIFE

We have the full text of his message at Mary's funeral and we have his own recollections of this loss. To feel the force of what he said, we have to know that they loved each other deeply and enjoyed each other in the work they shared:

> Were we happy? Verily we were. With every year our happiness increased more and more. I never saw my beloved wife at any time, when I met her unexpectedly anywhere in Bristol, without being delighted so to do. I never met her even in the Orphan Houses, without my heart being delighted so to do. Day by day, as we met in our dressing room, at the Orphan Houses, to wash our hands before dinner and tea, I was delighted to meet her, and she was equally pleased to see me. Thousands of times I told her—"My darling, I never saw you at any time, since you became my wife, without my being delighted to see you."[30]

---

[28] Ibid., 2:389–401.
[29] Pierson, *George Müller*, 279.
[30] Müller, *A Narrative*, 2:392–93.

Then came the diagnosis: "When I heard what Mr. Pritchard's judgment was, viz., that the malady was rheumatic fever, I naturally expected the worst. . . . My heart was nigh to be broken on account of the depth of my affection."[31] The one who had seen God answer ten thousand prayers for the support of the orphan did not get what he asked this time. Or did he?

Twenty minutes after four on the Lord's Day, February 6, 1870, Mary died. "I fell on my knees and thanked God for her release, and for having taken her to Himself, and asked the Lord to help and support us."[32] He recalled later how he strengthened himself during these hours. And here we see the key to his life:

> The last portion of Scripture which I read to my precious wife was this: "The Lord God is a sun and shield, the Lord will give grace and glory, no good thing will he withhold from them that walk uprightly." Now, if we have believed in the Lord Jesus Christ, we have received grace, we are partakers of grace, and to all such he will give glory also. I said to myself, with regard to the latter part, "no good thing will he withhold from them that walk uprightly"—I am in myself a poor worthless sinner, but I have been saved by the blood of Christ; and I do not live in sin, I walk uprightly before God. Therefore, if it is really good for me, my darling wife will be raised up again; sick as she is. God will restore her again. But if she is not restored again, then it would not be a good thing for me. And so my heart was at rest. I was satisfied with God. And all this springs, as I have often said before, from taking God at his word, believing what he says.[33]

Here is the cluster of unshakable convictions and experiences that are the key to Müller's remarkable life. "I am in myself a poor worth-

---

[31] Ibid., 2:398.
[32] Ibid., 2:400.
[33] Ibid., 2:745. In the actual funeral sermon, Müller took as a text Psalm 119:68, "Thou art good, and doest good" (KJV). He opened it like this: "'The Lord is good, and doeth good,' all will be according to His own blessed character. Nothing but that, which is good, like Himself, can proceed from Him. If he pleases to take my dearest wife, it will be good, like Himself. What I have to do, as His child, is to be satisfied with what my Father does, that I may glorify Him. After this my soul not only aimed, but this, my soul, by God's grace, attained to. I was satisfied with God." Ibid., 2:398–99.

less sinner." "I have been saved by the blood of Christ." "I do not live in sin." "God is sovereign over life and death. If it is good for her and for me, she will be restored again. If it is not, she won't." "My heart is at rest." "I am satisfied with God."

All this comes from taking God at his word. There you see the innermost being of George Müller and the key to his life—the Word of God, revealing his sin, revealing his Savior, revealing God's sovereignty, revealing God's goodness, revealing God's promise, awakening his faith, satisfying his soul. "I was satisfied with God."

THE GIFT OF FAITH VS. THE GRACE OF FAITH

So, were his prayers for Mary answered? To understand how Müller himself would answer this question, we have to see the way he distinguished between the extraordinary *gift* of faith and the more ordinary *grace* of faith. He constantly insisted, when people put him on a pedestal, that he did *not* have the gift of faith just because he would pray for his own needs and the needs of the orphans, and the money would arrive in remarkable ways:

> Think not, dear reader, that I have *the gift of faith*, that is, that gift of which we read in 1 Corinthians 12:9, and which is mentioned along with "the gifts of healing," "the working of miracles," "prophecy," and that on that account I am able to trust in the Lord. *It is true* that the faith, which I am enabled to exercise, is altogether God's own gift; it is true that He alone supports it, and that He alone can increase it; it is true that, moment by moment, I depend upon Him for it, and that, if I were only one moment left to myself, my faith would utterly fail; but *it is not true* that my faith is that gift of faith which is spoken of in 1 Corinthians 12:9.[34]

The reason he is so adamant about this is that his whole life—especially in the way he supported the orphans by faith and prayer without asking anyone but God for money—was consciously planned to

---

[34] Ibid., 1:302. The italics are Müller's.

encourage Christians that God could really be trusted to meet their needs. We will never understand Müller's passion for the orphan ministry if we don't see that the good of the orphans was second to this.

> The three chief reasons for establishing an Orphan-House are: 1) That God may be glorified, should He be pleased to furnish me with the means, in its being seen that it is not a vain thing to trust in Him; and that thus the faith of His children may be strengthened. 2) The spiritual welfare of fatherless and motherless children. 3) Their temporal welfare.[35]

Make no mistake about it: the order of those three goals is intentional. He makes that explicit over and over in his *Narrative*: *the orphan houses exist to display that God can be trusted and to encourage believers to take him at his word.* This was a deep sense of calling with Müller. He said that God had given him the mercy of "being able to take God by His word and to rely upon it."[36] He was grieved that "so many believers . . . were harassed and distressed in mind, or brought guilt on their consciences, on account of not trusting in the Lord."[37] This grace that he had to trust God's promises, and this grief that so many believers didn't trust his promises, shaped Müller's entire life. This was his supreme passion: *to display with open proofs that God could be trusted with the practical affairs of life.* This was the higher aim of building the orphan houses and supporting them by asking God, not people, for money:

> It seemed to me best done, by the establishing of an Orphan-House. It needed to be something which could be seen, even by the natural eye. Now, if I, a poor man, simply by prayer and faith, obtained, without asking any individual, the means for establishing and carrying on an Orphan-House: there would be something which, with the Lord's blessing, might be instrumental in strengthening the faith of the children of God besides being a testimony to the consciences of the unconverted, of the reality of the things of God. This,

---

[35] Ibid., 1:103.
[36] Ibid., 1:105.
[37] Müller, *Autobiography*, 148.

then, was *the primary reason*, for establishing the Orphan-House. . . .
The *first and primary object* of the work was, (and still is) that God
might be magnified by the fact, that the orphans under my care are
provided, with all they need, only by prayer and faith, without any
one being asked by me or my fellow-laborers, whereby it may be
seen, that God is FAITHFUL STILL and HEARS PRAYER STILL.[38]

That was the chief passion and unifying aim of Müller's ministry: *to
live a life and lead a ministry in a way that proves God is real, God is trustworthy, and God answers prayer.* He built orphanages the way he did to help
Christians trust God. He says it over and over again.[39]

Now we see why he was so adamant that his faith was *not* the gift
of faith mentioned in 1 Corinthians 12:9, which only some people
have, but was the grace of faith that all Christians should have.[40] Now
we are ready to see this crucial distinction he made between the gift
of faith and the grace of faith. His entire aim in life hung on this. If
Christians simply say, "Müller is in a class by himself; he has the gift
of faith," then we are all off the hook and he is no longer a prod and
proof and inspiration for how we ought to live. Here is what he says:

The difference between the *gift* and the *grace* of faith seems to me
this. According to the *gift* of faith I am able to do a thing, or believe
that a thing will come to pass, the not doing of which, or the not
believing of which would not be sin; according to the *grace* of faith
I am able to do a thing, or believe that a thing will come to pass, respecting which I have the word of God as the ground to rest upon,
and, therefore, the not doing it, or the not believing it would be
sin. For instance, the gift of faith would be needed, to believe that
a sick person should be restored again though there is no human
probability: for there is no promise to that effect; the grace of faith
is needed to believe that the Lord will give me the necessaries of

---

[38] Müller, *A Narrative*, 1:105. Italics added. The capital letters are his.
[39] Ibid., 1:131, 250, 285, 317, 443, 486, 548, 558, etc.
[40] "All believers are called upon, in the simple confidence of faith, to cast all their burdens upon Him, to trust in Him for every thing, and not only to make every thing a subject of prayer, but to expect answers to their petitions which they have asked according to His will, and in the name of the Lord Jesus." Ibid., 1:302.

life, if I first seek the kingdom of God and His righteousness: for there is a promise to that effect. Matthew 6:33.[41]

Müller did not think he had any biblical ground for being certain that God would spare his wife Mary. He admits that a few times in his life he was given "something like the gift (not grace) of faith so that unconditionally I could ask and look for an answer,"[42] but he did not have that rare gift in Mary's case. And so he prayed for her healing conditionally—namely, if it would be good for them and for God's glory. But most deeply he prayed that they would be satisfied in God, whatever God did. And God did answer that prayer by helping Müller believe Psalm 84:11: "No good thing will God withhold." God withheld no good thing from him, and he was satisfied with God's sovereign will. All this, he says, "springs . . . from taking God at his word, believing what he says."[43]

How Did Müller Get to This Position?

Let's go back and let Müller tell the story—essential parts of which are omitted from all the biographies I have looked at.

His father was an unbeliever, and George grew up a liar and a thief, by his own testimony.[44] His mother died when he was fourteen, and he records no impact that this loss had on him except that while she was dying he was roving the streets with his friends, "half intoxicated."[45] He went on living a bawdy life, then found himself in prison for stealing when he was sixteen years old. His father paid to get him out, beat him, and took him to live in another town (Schoenbeck). Müller used his academic skills to make money by tutoring in Latin, French, and mathematics. Finally his father sent him to the University of Halle to study divinity and prepare for the ministry

---

[41] Ibid., 1:65.
[42] Ibid.
[43] Ibid., 2:745.
[44] Ibid., 1:10.
[45] Ibid.

because that would be a good living. Neither he nor George had any spiritual aspirations. Of the nine hundred divinity students in Halle, Müller later estimated that maybe nine feared the Lord.[46]

Then, on a Saturday afternoon in the middle of November 1825, when Müller was twenty years old, he was invited to a Bible study and, by the grace of God, felt the desire to go. "It was to me as if I had found something after which I had been seeking all my life long. I immediately wished to go."[47] "They read the Bible, sang, prayed, and read a printed sermon."[48] To his amazement, Müller said, "the whole made a deep impression on me. I was happy; though, if I had been asked, why I was happy I could not have clearly explained it. . . . I have not the least doubt, that on that evening, [God] began a work of grace in me. . . . That evening was the turning point in my life."[49]

That's true. But there was another turning point four years later that the biographies do not open for the reader, but which, for Müller, was absolutely decisive in shaping the way he viewed God and the way he did ministry.

A Decisive Turning Point: Confidence in the Sovereign Goodness of God

He came to England in the hope of being a missionary with the London Missionary Society. Soon he found his theology and ministry convictions turning away from the LMS, until there was a break. In the meantime, a momentous encounter happened.

Müller became sick (thank God for providential sickness!), and in the summer of 1829, he went for recovery to a town called Teignmouth. There, in a little chapel called Ebenezer, he made at least two crucial discoveries: the preciousness of reading and meditating on

---

[46] Ibid., 1:16.
[47] Ibid., 1:17.
[48] Ibid., 1:16.
[49] Ibid., 1:17.

the Word of God[50] and the truth of the doctrines of grace.[51] For ten days Müller lived with a nameless man who changed his life forever: "Through the instrumentality of this brother, the Lord bestowed a great blessing upon me, for which I shall have cause to thank Him throughout eternity."[52]

> Before this period I had been much opposed to the doctrines of election, particular redemption, and final persevering grace; so much so that, a few days after my arrival at Teignmouth, I called election a devilish doctrine. . . . I knew nothing about the choice of God's people, and did not believe that the child of God, when once made so, was safe for ever. . . . But now I was brought to examine these precious truths by the word of God.[53]

Müller was led to embrace the doctrines of grace—the robust, mission-minded, soul-winning, orphan-loving Calvinism that marked William Carey, who died in 1834, and that would mark Charles Spurgeon, who was born in 1834. The doctrines changed his life. They had a profound effect on the holiness of his behavior:

> Being made willing to have no glory of my own in the conversion of sinners, but to consider myself merely as an instrument; and being made willing to receive what the Scriptures said; I went to the Word, reading the New Testament from the beginning, with a particular reference to these truths. To my great astonishment I found that the passages which speak decidedly for election and persevering grace, were about four times as many as those which speak apparently against these truths; and even those few, shortly after, when I had examined and understood them, served to confirm me in the above doctrines.

---

[50] "For when it pleased the Lord in August, 1829, to bring me really to the Scriptures, my life and walk became *very* different." Ibid., 1:28–29.

[51] "Between July, 1829, and January, 1830, I had seen the leading truths connected with the second coming of our Lord Jesus; I had apprehended the all-sufficiency of the Holy Scriptures as our rule, and the Holy Spirit as our teacher; I had seen clearly the precious doctrines of the grace of God, about which I had been uninstructed for nearly four years after my conversion." Ibid., 2:720.

[52] Ibid., 1:39.

[53] Ibid., 1:46.

As to the effect which my belief in these doctrines had on me, I am constrained to state, for God's glory, that though I am still exceedingly weak, and by no means so dead to the lusts of the flesh, and the lust of the eyes, and the pride of life, as I might and as I ought to be, yet, by the grace of God, I have walked more closely with Him since that period. My life has not been so variable, and I may say that I have lived much more for God than before.[54]

About forty years later, in 1870, Müller spoke to some young believers about the importance of what had happened to him at Teignmouth. He said that his preaching had been fruitless for four years from 1825 to 1829 in Germany, but then he came to England and was taught the doctrines of grace:

In the course of time I came to this country, and it pleased God then to show to me the doctrines of grace in a way in which I had not seen them before. At first I hated them, "If this were true *I* could do nothing at all in the conversion of sinners, as all would depend upon God and the working of His Spirit." But when it pleased God to reveal these truths to me, and my heart was brought to such a state that I could say, "I am not only content simply to be a hammer, an axe, or a saw, in God's hands; but I shall count it an honor to be taken up and used by Him in any way; and if sinners are converted through my instrumentality, from my inmost soul I will give Him all the glory"; the Lord gave me to see fruit; the Lord gave me to see fruit in abundance; sinners were converted by scores; and ever since God has used me in one way or other in His service.[55]

ASKING GOD (AND USING MEANS)
TO MOVE MEN'S HEARTS

This discovery of the all-encompassing sovereignty of God became the foundation of Müller's confidence in God to answer his prayers

---

[54] Ibid. "Thus, I say, the electing love of God in Christ (when I have been able to *realize it*) has often been the means of producing holiness, instead of leading me into sin." Ibid., 1:40.
[55] Ibid., 1:752.

for money. He gave up his regular salary.[56] He refused to ask people
directly for money:

> [The gifts have been given to me] without one single individual
> having been asked by me for any thing. The reason why I have
> refrained altogether from soliciting any one for help is, that the
> hand of God evidently might be seen in the matter, that thus my
> fellow-believers might be encouraged more and more to trust in
> Him, and that also those who know not the Lord, may have a fresh
> proof that, indeed, it is not a vain thing to pray to God.[57]

He prayed and published his reports about the goodness of God
and the answers to his prayer. These yearly reports were circulated
around the world, and they clearly had a huge effect in motivating
people to give to the orphan work.

Müller walked a narrow line: on the one hand, he wanted to give
God all the credit for answering prayer for meeting all his needs, and
so he did not ask people directly for help. But on the other hand, he
wanted this work of God to be known so that Christians would be encouraged to trust God for answered prayer. But in the very publication
of the work of God, he was making known how much he depended on
the generosity of God's people, and thus motivating them by human
means to give.

Müller knew that God used means. In fact, he loved to say, "Work
with all your might; but trust not in the least in your work."[58] He was
open and unashamed in saying that the reports of God's provision
motivated people to give:

---

[56] "Upon our first coming to Bristol we declined accepting anything in the shape of regular salary. . . .
We did not act thus because we thought it wrong that those who were ministered unto in spiritual
things should minister unto us in temporal things; but . . . because we would not have the liberality
of the brethren to be a matter of constraint, but willingly." Ibid., 1:275.

[57] Ibid., 1:132.

[58] Ibid., 1:611. "This is one of the great secrets in connexion with successful service for the Lord; to
work as if everything depended upon our diligence, and yet not to rest in the least upon our *exertions*,
but upon the blessing of the Lord." Ibid., 2:290. "Speak also for the Lord, as if everything depended
on your exertions; yet trust not in the least in your exertions, but in the Lord, who *alone* can cause
your efforts to be made effectual." Ibid., 2:279.

I do not mean to say that God does not use the Reports as instruments in procuring us means. They are written in order that I may thus give an account of my stewardship, but particularly, in order that, by these printed accounts of the work, the chief end of this Institution may be answered, which is to raise another public testimony to an unbelieving world, that in these last days the Living God is still the Living God, listening to the prayers of His children, and helping those who put their trust in Him; and in order that believers generally may be benefited and especially be encouraged to trust in God for everything they may need, and be stirred up to deal in greater simplicity with God respecting everything connected with their own particular position and circumstances; in short, that the children of God may be brought to the practical use of the Holy Scriptures, as the word of the Living God.—But while these are the primary reasons for publishing these Reports, we doubt not that the Lord has again and again used them as instruments in leading persons to help us with their means.[59]

But he also insisted that his hope was in God alone, not his exertions and not the published reports. These means could not account for the remarkable answers that he received.

SOVEREIGN GOODNESS

Müller's faith that his prayers for money would be answered was rooted in the sovereignty of God. When faced with a crisis in having the means to pay a bill, he would say, "*How* the means are to come, I know not; but I know that God is almighty, that the hearts of all are in His hands, and that, if He pleaseth to influence persons, they will send help."[60] That was the root of his confidence: *God is almighty, the hearts of all men are in his hands,*[61] *and when God chooses to influence their hearts, they will give.*

---

[59] Ibid., 1:662.
[60] Ibid., 1:594.
[61] "There is scarcely a country, from whence I have not received donations; yet all come unsolicited, often anonymously, and in by far the greater number of cases from entire strangers, who are led by God, in answer to our prayers, to help on this work which was commenced, and is carried on, only in

He had come to know and love this absolute sovereignty of God in the context of the doctrines of *grace*, and therefore he cherished it mainly as sovereign *goodness*.[62] This gave him a way to maintain a personal peace beyond human understanding in the midst of tremendous stress and occasional tragedy. "The Lord never lays more on us," he said, "in the way of chastisement, than our state of heart makes needful; so that whilst He smites with the one hand, He supports with the other."[63] In the face of painful circumstances, he said, "I bow, I am satisfied with the will of my Heavenly Father, I seek by perfect submission to His holy will to glorify Him, I kiss continually the hand that has thus afflicted me."[64]

And when he was about to lose a piece of property that he wanted for the next orphan house, he said, "If the Lord were to take this piece of land from me, *it would be only for the purpose of giving me a still better one; for our Heavenly Father never takes any earthly thing from His children except He means to give them something better instead.*"[65] This is what I mean by confidence in God's sovereign goodness. This confidence was the root of Müller's faith and ministry.

The Aroma of Müller's Calvinism: Satisfaction and Glad Self-Denial

But there was an aroma about Müller's Calvinism that was different from many stereotypes. For him, the sovereign goodness of God served, first and foremost, the satisfaction of the soul. And then the satisfied soul was freed to sacrifice and live a life of simplicity and risk and self-denial and love. But everything flowed from the soul that was first satisfied in the gracious, sovereign God. Müller is clearer on

---

dependence on the Living God, in whose hands are the hearts of all men." Ibid., 2:387. "Our Heavenly Father has the hearts of all men at His disposal, and we give ourselves to prayer to Him, and He, in answer to *our* prayers, lays the necessities of this work on the hearts of his stewards." Ibid., 2:498. "We should not trust in the Reports, and expect that they would bring in something, but trust in the Living God, who has the hearts of all in His hands, and to whom all the gold and silver belongs." Ibid., 2:80.
[62] "Remember also, that God delights to bestow blessing, but, generally, as the result of earnest, believing prayer." Ibid., 2:279.
[63] Ibid., 1:61.
[64] Ibid., 2:401.
[65] Ibid., 1:505. The italics are Müller's.

this than anyone I have ever read. He is unashamed to sound almost childishly simple:

> According to my judgment the most important point to be attended to is this: above all things see to it that your souls are happy in the Lord. Other things may press upon you, the Lord's work may even have urgent claims upon your attention, but I deliberately repeat, it is of supreme and paramount importance that you should seek above all things to have your souls truly happy in God Himself! Day by day seek to make this the most important business of your life. This has been my firm and settled condition for the last five and thirty years. For the first four years after my conversion I knew not its vast importance, but now after much experience I specially commend this point to the notice of my younger brethren and sisters in Christ: the secret of all true effectual service is joy in God, having experimental acquaintance and fellowship with God Himself.[66]

Why is this the "most important" thing? Why is daily happiness in God "of supreme and paramount importance"? One answer he gives is that it glorifies God. After telling about one of his wife's illnesses when he almost lost her, he says, "I have . . . stated this case so fully, to show the deep importance to be satisfied with the will of God, not only for the sake of glorifying Him, but as the best way, in the end, of having given to us the desire of our hearts."[67] Being satisfied in God is "of supreme and paramount importance" because it glorifies God. It shows that God is gloriously satisfying.

But there is another answer, namely, that happiness in God is the only source of durable and God-honoring self-denial and sacrifice and love. In reference to lifestyle changes and simplicity, he says:

> We should begin the thing in a right way, *i.e.* aim after the right state of heart; begin *inwardly* instead of *outwardly*. If otherwise, it

---

[66] Ibid., 2:730–31. "I saw more clearly than ever, that the first great and primary business to which I ought to attend every day was, to have my soul happy in the Lord. The first thing to be concerned about was not, how much I might serve the Lord, how I might glorify the Lord; but how I might get my soul into a happy state, and how *my* inner man might be nourished." Ibid., 1:271.

[67] Ibid., 2:406.

will not last. We shall look back, or even get into a worse state than we were before. But oh! how different if joy in God leads us to any little act of self denial. How gladly do we do it then![68]

"Glad self-denial" is the aroma of Müller's Calvinism. How can there be such a thing? He answers: "Self-denial is not so much an *impoverishment* as a *postponement*: we make a sacrifice of a present good for the sake of a future and greater good."[69] Therefore, happiness in God is of "supreme importance" because it is the key to love that sacrifices and takes risks. "Whatever be done . . . in the way of giving up, or self-denial, or deadness to the world, should result from the joy we have in God."[70]

A well-to-do woman visited him once to discuss a possible gift to the Institution. He did not ask her for the money. But when she was gone, he asked God for it. And the way he did reveals his understanding of how the human heart works:

> After she was gone, I asked the Lord, that He would be pleased to make this dear sister so happy in Himself and enable her so to realize her true riches and inheritance in the Lord Jesus, and the reality of her heavenly calling, that she might be constrained by the love of Christ, cheerfully to lay down this 500 [pounds] at His feet.[71]

How Do We Get and Keep Our Happiness in God?

If happiness in God is "of supreme and paramount importance" because it is the spring of sacrificial love that honors God, then the crucial question becomes, how do we get it and keep it?

> But in what way shall we attain to this settled happiness of soul? How shall we learn to enjoy God? How obtain such an all-sufficient soul-satisfying portion in him as shall *enable us to let go the things of this world* as vain and worthless in comparison? I answer, This

---

[68] Ibid., 1:355.
[69] Cited in Pierson, *George Müller*, 374.
[70] Müller, *A Narrative*, 1:355.
[71] Ibid., 1:326.

happiness is to be obtained through the study of the Holy Scriptures. God has therein revealed Himself unto us in the face of Jesus Christ.[72]

Happiness in God comes from seeing God revealed to us in the face of Jesus Christ through the Scriptures. "In them . . . we become acquainted with the character of God. Our eyes are divinely opened to see what a lovely Being God is! And this good, gracious, loving, heavenly Father is ours, our portion for time and for eternity."[73] Knowing God is the key to being happy in God:

> The more we know of God, the happier we are. . . . When we became a little acquainted with God . . . our true happiness . . . commenced; and the more we become acquainted with him, the more truly happy we become. What will make us so exceedingly happy in heaven? It will be the fuller knowledge of God.[74]

Therefore, the most crucial means of fighting for joy in God is to immerse oneself in the Scriptures, where we see God in Christ most clearly. When he was seventy-one years old, Müller spoke to younger believers:

> Now in brotherly love and affection I would give a few hints to my younger fellow-believers as to the way in which to keep up spiritual enjoyment. It is absolutely needful in order that happiness in the Lord may continue, that the Scriptures be regularly read. These are God's appointed means for the nourishment of the inner man. . . . Consider it, and ponder over it. . . . Especially we should read regularly through the Scriptures, consecutively, and not pick out here and there a chapter. If we do, we remain spiritual dwarfs. I tell you so affectionately. For the first four years after my conversion I made no progress, because I neglected the Bible. But when I regularly read on through the whole with reference to my own heart and soul, I

---

[72] Ibid., 2:731.
[73] Ibid., 2:732.
[74] Ibid., 2:740.

directly made progress. Then my peace and joy continued more and more. Now I have been doing this for 47 years. I have read through the whole Bible about 100 times and I always find it fresh when I begin again. Thus my peace and joy have increased more and more.[75]

Müller was seventy-one, and he would live and read on for another twenty-one years. But he never changed his strategy for satisfaction in God. When he was seventy-six, he wrote the same thing he did when he was sixty, "I saw more clearly than ever, that the first great and primary business to which I ought to attend every day was, to have my soul happy in the Lord."[76] And the means stayed the same:

> I saw that the most important thing I had to do was to give myself to the reading of the word of God, and to meditation on it. . . . What is the food of the inner man? Not *prayer*, but *the word of God*; and . . . not the simple reading of the word of God, so that it only passes through our minds, just as water runs through a pipe, but considering what we read, pondering over it, and applying it to our hearts.[77]

This brings us back to the satisfaction of Müller's soul at the death of his wife, Mary. Remember, he said: "My heart was at rest. I was satisfied with God. And all this springs, as I have often said before, from taking God at his word, believing what he says."[78]

The aim of George Müller's life was to glorify God by helping people take God at his word.[79] To that end, he saturated his soul with the Word of God. At one point, he said that he read the Bible five or ten times more than he read any other books.[80] His aim was to see God in Jesus Christ crucified and risen from the dead in order that he might maintain the happiness of his soul in God. By this deep satisfaction in God, Müller was set free from the fears and lusts of the world.

---

[75] Ibid., 2:834.
[76] Ibid., 1:271.
[77] Ibid., 1:272–73.
[78] Ibid., 2:745.
[79] "I have not served a hard Master, and that is what I delight to show. For, to speak well of His name, that thus my beloved fellow-pilgrims, who may read this, may be encouraged to trust in Him, is the chief purpose of my writing." Ibid., 1:63.
[80] Ibid., 1:101.

And in this freedom of love, he chose a strategy of ministry and style of life that put the reality and trustworthiness and beauty of God on display. To use his own words, his life became a "visible proof to the unchangeable faithfulness of the Lord."[81]

Müller was sustained in this extraordinary life by his deep convictions that God is sovereign over the human heart and can turn it where he wills in answer to prayer; that God is sovereign over life and death; and that God is good in his sovereignty and withholds no good thing from those who walk uprightly. He strengthened himself continually in his wife's final illness with the words of a hymn:

> Best of blessings He'll provide us,
> Nought but good shall e'er betide us,
> Safe to glory He will guide us,
> Oh how He loves![82]

An Exhortation and Plea

I will let Müller have the closing word of exhortation and pleading for us to join him in the path of radical, joyful faith:

> My dear Christian reader, will you not try this way? Will you not know for yourself . . . the preciousness and the happiness of this way of casting all your cares and burdens and necessities upon God? This way is as open to you as to me. . . . Every one is invited and commanded to trust in the Lord, to trust in Him with all his heart, and to cast his burden upon Him, and to call upon Him in the day of trouble. Will you not do this, my dear brethren in Christ? I long that you may do so. I desire that you may taste the sweetness of that state of heart, in which, while surrounded by difficulties and necessities, you can yet be at peace, because you know that the living God, your Father in heaven, cares for you.[83]

---

[81] Ibid., 1:105.
[82] Ibid., 2:399.
[83] Ibid., 1:521.

It is *only* in the trial of GOD's grace that its *beauty and power* can be seen. Then all our trials of temper, circumstances, provocation, sickness, disappointment, bereavement, will but give a higher burnish to the mirror, and enable us to reflect more fully and more perfectly the glory and blessedness of our MASTER.

Hudson Taylor

3

HUDSON TAYLOR

An Enduring and Expansive Enjoyment
of Union with Jesus Christ

Our focus in this chapter will be on how Hudson Taylor experienced union with Christ. The warning flags go up immediately, because it is well known that Taylor was significantly influenced by the Keswick Movement and its views of sanctification, which, in the worst exponents, are seriously flawed. My conclusion is that Taylor was *not* one of those worst exponents, and that he was protected from Keswick's worst flaws by his allegiance to the Bible, his experience of lifelong suffering and sorrow, and his belief in the sovereignty of God.[1]

THERE IS MORE OF GOD YET TO BE ENJOYED

All of this means that there are glorious things to see in the life of Hudson Taylor and wonderful lessons to be learned about abiding in Christ and about faith and prayer and obedience and suffering.

---

[1] It is important to note that Keswick teaching has changed considerably in recent decades. As Andy Naselli writes: "Beginning in the 1920s, the Keswick Convention's view of sanctification began to shift from the view promoted by the leaders of the early convention. William Scroggie (1877–1958) led that transformation to a view of sanctification closer to the Reformed view. The official Keswick Convention that now hosts the annual Keswick conferences holds a Reformed view of sanctification and invites speakers who are confessionally reformed." Andrew D. Naselli, "Why 'Let Go and Let God' Is a Bad Idea," *Tabletalk*, October 2011, 74.

Whatever else Keswick's teaching may have gotten wrong, it was not wrong to say to all Christians that there is more joy, more peace, more love, more power, and more fruit to be enjoyed in Christ than we are presently enjoying.

- 1 Thessalonians 4:1—"As you received from us how you ought to walk and to please God, just as you are doing, . . . do so *more and more*."
- 1 Thessalonians 4:9–10—"Concerning brotherly love . . . we urge you, brothers, to do this *more and more*."
- Philippians 1:9—"It is my prayer that your love may abound *more and more*."
- Ephesians 5:18–19—"Be *filled* with the Spirit, addressing one another in psalms and hymns and spiritual songs, singing and making melody to the Lord with your heart."
- 1 Peter 1:2—"May grace and peace *be multiplied* to you."
- And most amazing of all: Ephesians 3:16–19—"According to the riches of his glory, . . . may [the Father] grant you to be strengthened with power through his Spirit in your inner being, so that Christ may dwell in your hearts through faith—that you, being rooted and grounded in love, may have strength to comprehend with all the saints what is the breadth and length and height and depth, and to know the love of Christ that surpasses knowledge, that you may be *filled with all the fullness of God*."

Any view of the Christian life that does not promote the desire for, and the pursuit of, this inexpressible fullness—this more—is as defective as the view that says its usual way of coming is through a single crisis experience of full consecration.

A PRAYER FOR THE READER

The link between Taylor's pursuit of this fullness and the legacy of the China Inland Mission is enormously instructive. It is relevant for everyone who wants to experience the peace that passes all understanding (Phil. 4:7). It is relevant for any one of you who wants to see your life bear fruit wonderfully out of proportion with your limitations.

That is what I hope God does with this story of Hudson Taylor: lead you into a deeper experience of union with Christ and inspire you to venture more for his glory than you ever have.

When Taylor wrote one of his most famous sayings, "Depend upon it, GOD's work done in GOD's way will never lack GOD's supplies,"[2] he meant every kind of need that we have—money and health and faith and peace and strength. And that is my prayer for this chapter: that you will see and experience new possibilities for your life—more faith, more joy, more peace, more love, and all the money you need to do his will—which may be none.

And all of that is because of your union with Christ, as is put so well in one of Taylor's favorite texts: "My God will supply every need of yours according to his riches in glory *in Christ Jesus*" (Phil. 4:19). And then, because of all that, I pray you will launch into some venture, some dream of ministry, beyond all your real or perceived inadequacies, for the glory of Christ.

He Was Not a Short-Lived Meteorite

Unlike Robert and Hannah Smith, who were among those who gave early influence to Keswick thinking, Taylor did not make shipwreck of his faith. From his conversion to his death at age seventy-three in 1905, he was unwavering in his allegiance to Jesus Christ and Christ's purpose to evangelize all the provinces of China. Whatever his views of the Christian life, they served him well, and the legacy of his stead-fast faith and obedience and fruitfulness is astonishing. He did not have a flashy experience and then fade away. He had an experience indeed, and then he proved Christ over and over, as the old song says:

---

[2] Cited in Frederick Howard Taylor and Geraldine Taylor, *Hudson Taylor and the China Inland Mission: The Growth of a Work of God* (Littleton, CO; Mississauga, ON; Kent, TN: OMF Books, 1995), 42.

"Jesus, Jesus, how I trust Him, How I've proved Him o'er and o'er."[3]
So his life is worth looking at.

A DRAMATIC CONVERSION

Hudson Taylor was born May 21, 1832, at Barnsley, England, into a devout Methodist home. At the age of seventeen, he was dramatically converted through the prayers of his mother. His friend Charles Spurgeon tells the story dramatically. Spurgeon was two years younger than Taylor, and, as we have seen, a great admirer of Taylor's faith and zeal for the gospel. They knew each other from at least 1864, when Taylor took his wife, Maria, and Wang Lae-djün to the Metropolitan Tabernacle. Spurgeon invited him to address a weekday meeting and to give a lecture on China. "A mutual admiration which never faded grew from that beginning."[4] Here's how Spurgeon weaves the story of his friend's conversion into one of his sermons:

> Oh, that some here may have faith to claim at this moment the salvation of their friends! May desire be wrought into expectancy, and hope become certainty! Like Jacob at Jabbok, may we lay hold of God, saying, "I will not let thee go, except thou bless me." To such faith the Lord will give a quick response. He that will not be denied shall not be denied.
>
> My friend, Hudson Taylor, who has done such a wonderful work for China, is an instance of this. Brought up in a godly home, he, as a young man, tried to imitate the lives of his parents, and failing in his own strength to make himself better, he swung to the other extreme, and began to entertain skeptical notions. One day, when his mother was from home, a great yearning after her boy possessed her, and she went up to her room to plead with God that "even now" he would save him. If I remember aright, she said that she would not leave the room until she had the assurance that her boy would be brought to Christ.

---

[3] From the hymn "'Tis So Sweet to Trust in Jesus" by Louisa M. R. Stead, 1882.
[4] Alvyn Austin, *China's Millions: The China Inland Mission and Late Qing Society, 1832–1905* (Grand Rapids, MI: Eerdmans, 2007), 87.

At length her faith triumphed, and she rose quite certain that all was well, and that "even now" her son was saved. What was he doing at that time? Having half an hour to spare, he wandered into his father's library, and aimlessly took down one book after another to find some short and interesting passage to divert his mind. He could not find what he wanted in any of the books; so, seeing a narrative tract, he took it up with the intention of reading the story, and putting it down when the sermon part of it began. As he read, he came to the words "the finished work of Christ", and almost at the very moment in which his mother, who was miles away, claimed his soul of God, light came into his heart. He saw that it was by the finished work of Christ that he was to be saved; and kneeling in his father's library, he sought and found the life of God.

Some days afterwards, when his mother returned, he said to her, "I have some news to tell you." "Oh, I know what it is!" she answered, smiling, "You have given yourself to God." "Who told you?" he asked, in astonishment. "God told me," she said, and together they praised him, who, at the same moment, gave the faith to the mother, and the life to the son, and who has since made him such a blessing to the world. It was the mother's faith, claiming the blessing "even now", that did it. I tell you this remarkable incident that many others may be stirred up to the same immediate and importunate desire for the salvation of their children and relatives. There are some things we must always pray for with submission as to whether it is the will of God to bestow them upon us: but for the salvation of men and women we may ask without a fear. God delights to save and to bless; and when the faith is given to us to expect an immediate answer to such a prayer, thrice happy are we. Seek such faith even now, I beseech you, "even now."[5]

The newly converted Taylor was at first part of the Wesleyan Methodist Connection, the church of his family. But his independent,

---

[5]C. H. Spurgeon, *The Metropolitan Tabernacle Pulpit Sermons*, vol. 38 (London: Passmore & Alabaster, 1892), 151–52.

Bible-oriented spirit showed itself very soon. In his application to the Chinese Evangelisation Society a year later, he wrote:

> At first I joined the Wesleyan Methodists, as my parents and friends were members of that body. But not being able to reconcile the late proceedings with the doctrines and precepts of Holy Scripture, I withdrew, and am at present united to the branch Society.[6]

Alvyn Austin comments:

> Having left the church of his fathers, Hudson Taylor . . . never "joined" another church, though he felt free to share communion with all. He was (re)baptized by the Plymouth Brethren and in a burst of enthusiasm, baptized his sister Amelia in a local stream. Later he was ordained by the Baptists, though this too was not publicized lest the CIM be identified with one church which would reduce its interdenominational appeal.[7]

No Debt, New Marriage

Within four years, Taylor was in China. During these four years, he entered rudimentary medical studies as an apprentice to Robert Hardey. Then, at the age of twenty-one, on September 19, 1853, he sailed for China with the Chinese Evangelisation Society. He had no formal training in theology or missions. Five and a half months later, he landed in Shanghai on March 1, 1854.

He learned the language quickly and, in his first two years in China, engaged in ten extended evangelistic journeys to the interior. But after four years, Taylor resigned from the Chinese Evangelisation Society because he had a deep conviction—shared with Spurgeon and George Müller—that borrowing money to sustain Christ's work was wrong:

---

[6] Cited in Austin, *China's Millions*, 47.
[7] Ibid. Even into the 1890s, the CIM was combatting rumors that it required members of the mission to be rebaptized as Baptists. Taylor replied, "'The statements you have heard of proselytism are entirely false. . . . Though a Baptist myself,' . . . the CIM had set aside certain districts for Baptists, Presbyterians, Anglicans, Methodists, and Plymouth Brethren." Cited in ibid., 342.

> To borrow money implied, to my mind, a contradiction of Scripture—a confession that GOD had withheld some good thing, and a determination to get for ourselves what He had not given. . . . To satisfy my conscience I was therefore compelled to resign connection with the Society which had hitherto supplied my salary.[8]

That was the beginning of a lifetime of never being in financial debt and never explicitly asking anyone for money[9]—following the lead of his hero, Müller.

On January 20, 1858, when he had been in China almost five years, Taylor married another missionary, Maria Dyer. They were married for twelve years. When Maria died at age thirty-three, she had given birth to eight children. Three died at birth and two in childhood, and the ones who lived to adulthood all became missionaries with the mission their father founded, the China Inland Mission.

THE BIRTH OF THE CHINA INLAND MISSION

In July 1860, two years into their marriage, Hudson and Maria sailed for England. He was seriously ill with hepatitis, but what seemed like a setback would soon give rise to the most decisive event of his life.[10] His burden for China grew for the next four years. He could not shake the idea that a new mission agency was needed. But he did not know if he could lead it. However, in the same period it took the Americans to fight the Civil War, God birthed in Taylor a dream that would change the history of the largest nation on earth. The moment came one Lord's Day on the beach near Brighton, England, which he describes like this:

> On Sunday, June 25th, 1865, unable to bear the sight of a congregation of a thousand or more Christian people rejoicing in their

---

[8] Cited in J. H. Taylor, *A Retrospect*, 3rd ed. (Toronto: China Inland Mission, n.d.), 99.
[9] "Inland China opened to the Gospel largely as an outcome of this life, . . . a mission which has never made an appeal for financial help, yet has never been in debt, that never asks man or woman to join its ranks." Dr. and Mrs. Howard Taylor, *Hudson Taylor's Spiritual Secret*, Kindle edition (May 25, 2013), 2.
[10] "Little did I then realize that this long absence from the work was a necessary step towards the formation of an agency that GOD would bless as He has blessed the China Inland Mission." Cited in M. G. Guinness, *The Story of the China Inland Mission*, 3rd ed. (London: Morgan & Scott, 1894), 1:193.

own security, while millions were perishing for lack of knowledge, I wandered out on the sands alone, in great spiritual agony; and there the LORD conquered my unbelief, and I surrendered myself to GOD for this service. I told Him that all the responsibility as to issues and consequences must rest with Him; that as His servant, it was mine to obey and to follow Him—His, to direct, to care for, and to guide me and those who might labour with me. Need I say that peace at once flowed into my burdened heart? There and then I asked Him for twenty-four fellow-workers, two for each of eleven inland provinces which were without a missionary, and two for Mongolia; and writing the petition on the margin of the Bible I had with me, I returned home with a heart enjoying rest such as it had been a stranger to for months.[11]

That was the birthplace of the China Inland Mission. Taylor was thirty-three years old. The missionaries were to have no guaranteed salaries, they were not to appeal for funds, and they were to adopt Chinese dress and press the gospel to the interior. On May 26, 1866, Hudson, Maria, and their children left England with the largest group of missionaries that had ever sailed to China—sixteen besides themselves. Taylor was to be the leader and settle all disputes.[12] Not everyone appreciated his leadership and the demands he made on himself and everyone else. One missionary accused him of tyranny and had to be dismissed.[13]

THE DECISIVE MOMENT

Three years later, after Taylor had experienced prolonged frustration with his own temptations and failures in holiness, the epoch-making

---

[11] Cited in J. H. Taylor, *A Retrospect*.

[12] "We came out as God's children at God's command [was Mr Taylor's simple statement] to do God's work, depending on Him for supplies; to wear native dress and to go inland. I was to be the leader in China. . . . There was no question as to who was to determine points at issue." Cited in Dr. and Mrs. Howard Taylor, *Hudson Taylor's Spiritual Secret*, 110.

[13] "Lewis Nicol, who accused Taylor of tyranny, had to be dismissed. Some CIM missionaries, in the wake of this and other controversies, left to join other missions, but in 1876, with 52 missionaries, CIM constituted one-fifth of the missionary force in China." *Hudson Taylor, Faith Missionary to China*, ChristianHistory.net, August 8, 2008, http://www.christianitytoday.com/ch/131christians/missionaries /htaylor.html?start=1.

experience happened—the one that stamps him as a part of the Keswick Movement.

Notice what he was experiencing leading up to the great change. He wrote to his mother:

> [The need for your prayer] has never been greater than at present. Envied by some, despised by many, hated by others, often blamed for things I never heard of or had nothing to do with, an innovator on what have become established rules of missionary practice, an opponent of mighty systems of heathen error and superstition, working without precedent in many respects and with few experienced helpers, often sick in body as well as perplexed in mind and embarrassed by circumstances—had not the Lord been specially gracious to me, had not my mind been sustained by the conviction that the work is His and that He is with me, . . . I must have fainted or broken down. But the battle is the Lord's, and He will conquer.
>
> We may fail—do fail continually—but He never fails. . . . I have continually to mourn that I follow at such a distance and learn so slowly to imitate my precious Master. I can not tell you how I am buffeted sometimes by temptation. I never knew how bad a heart I have. Yet I do know that I love God and love His work, and desire to serve Him only and in all things. And I value above all else that precious Saviour in whom alone I can be accepted. Often I am tempted to think that one so full of sin can not be a child of God at all. . . . May God help me to love Him more and serve Him better.[14]

The stage was set for the crisis that happened on September 4, 1869, in Zhenjiang. He exulted to one of his associates: "Oh, Mr. Judd, God has made me a new man! God has made me a new man!"[15] What happened that day was not ephemeral. He looked back almost thirty years later, giving thanks for the abiding experience of it:

> We shall never forget the blessing we received through the words, in John iv. 14, "Whosoever drinketh of the water that I shall give

---

[14] Cited in Dr. and Mrs. Howard Taylor, *Hudson Taylor's Spiritual Secret*, 140–41.

[15] Cited in Frederick Howard Taylor and Geraldine Taylor, *Hudson Taylor and the China Inland Mission*, 173.

him SHALL NEVER THIRST," nearly thirty years ago. As we realized that Christ literally meant what He said—that "shall" meant shall, and "never" meant never, and "thirst" meant thirst—our heart overflowed with joy as we accepted the gift. Oh, the thirst with which we had sat down, but oh, the joy with which we sprang from our seat, praising the Lord that the thirsting days were all past, and past for ever![16]

We should beware of being cynical here. Taylor was not naïve. He was speaking of a thirty-year-long experience in which he battled with some very low times. "The thirsting days were all past" does not mean he never had desires for Jesus again. It doesn't mean he never longed for more of Christ. We will turn to what it does mean shortly. But for now, we should simply be aware that, as his most thorough biographer wrote, his whole life "came to be revolutionized"[17] by this experience.

The Most Difficult Year of His Life

And just in time, too. The next year, 1870, was the most difficult of his life. His son Samuel died in January. Then in July, Maria gave birth to a son, Noel, who died two weeks later. And to crown Hudson's sorrows, on July 23, Maria died of cholera. She was thirty-three years old, and left the thirty-eight-year-old Hudson with four living children.

It was as though God had given Taylor his extraordinary experience of the all-satisfying Christ not as a kind of icing on the cake of conversion, but rather as a way of surviving and thriving in the worst of sorrows, which came to him almost immediately.

A New Marriage, a Life at Sea, a Loss of Life

A year later, Taylor sailed for England. While he was there, on November 28, 1871, he married the woman with whom he would spend

---

[16] Cited in James Hudson Taylor, *Separation and Service or Thoughts on Numbers VI, VII.*, Kindle edition, Locations 519–524.

[17] A. J. Broomhall, *The Shaping of Modern China: Hudson Taylor's Life and Legacy, Vol. 2 (1868–1990)* (Pasadena, CA: William Carey Library, Piquant Editions, 2005), 109 (originally published as vols. 5–7 of *Hudson Taylor and China's Open Century*).

nearly the rest of his life, Jennie Faulding. They were married for thirty-three years before she died in 1904, the year before he did. They had a son and a daughter besides the four children from Maria. During one period, from 1881 to 1890, Jennie was in England while Hudson traveled to China twice, separating them for a total of about six years.

In his lifetime, Taylor made ten voyages to China, which means, as I calculate it, that he spent between four and five years on the water in transit—a good reminder, I suppose, that he was a pilgrim here. Over time, his ministry became increasingly global as the ambassador for China and for the China Inland Mission. He was the general director from 1865 to 1902, when he handed over the role to Dixon Hoste.

Taylor lived to see the horrible Boxer Rebellion, which raged against all Christians and foreigners in China in 1900. The China Inland Mission lost more members than any other agency: fifty-eight adults and twenty-one children were killed. But the next year, when the allied nations were demanding compensation from the Chinese government, Taylor refused to accept payment for loss of property or life. His aim was to win the Chinese, not demand justice.

DEATH AND LEGACY

In February 1905, Taylor sailed for China for the last time. After a tour of some of the mission stations, he died on June 3 at Changsha, Hunan, at the age of seventy-three. He was buried at Chinkiang by the side of his first wife and the children who had died in China. This was not owing to a superior relationship to Maria, but to the distances involved. Jennie had died in Switzerland the year before. The cemetery in China was destroyed as part of the Cultural Revolution, and today industrial buildings stand over the site.

At the time of Taylor's death, the China Inland Mission was an international body with 825 missionaries living in all eighteen provinces of China; more than three hundred mission stations; more than five hundred local Chinese helpers; and twenty-five thousand

Christian converts.[18] Among the better-known luminaries who served China with CIM are the Cambridge Seven,[19] William Borden,[20] James Fraser,[21] and John and Betty Stam.[22]

Today, about sixteen hundred missionaries work for what is now known as OMF International.[23] Its international headquarters is in Singapore, and the mission is led by Patrick Fung, who is Chinese. The mission statement is: "We share the good news of Jesus Christ in all its fullness with East Asia's peoples to the glory of God." And the vision statement is: "Through God's grace, we aim to see an indigenous, biblical church movement in each people group of East Asia, evangelizing their own people and reaching out in mission to other peoples."

The year 2015 marked the 150th anniversary of the mission that Taylor founded. In 1900, there were one hundred thousand Christians in China, and today there are probably around 150 million.[24] This growth is God's work: one plants, another waters, but God gives the growth (1 Cor. 3:6). Nevertheless, it is the fruit of faithful labor. And Taylor labored longer and harder than most. That labor was sustained by union with Christ. So we turn to look at what this union meant for Taylor.

THE SENTENCE THAT REMOVED THE SCALES

On September 4, 1869, when he was thirty-seven years old, Taylor found a letter waiting for him at Zhenjiang from John McCarthy. God used the letter to revolutionize Taylor's life. "When my agony of soul was at its height, a sentence in a letter from dear McCarthy was used to

---

[18] Ralph R. Covell, "James Hudson Taylor: 1832–1905," *Biographical Dictionary of Chinese Christianity*, http://www.bdcconline.net/en/stories/t/taylor-james-hudson.php

[19] John Pollock, *The Cambridge Seven: The True Story of Ordinary Men Used in No Ordinary Way* (Fearn, Ross-Shire, Scotland: Christian Focus, 2006).

[20] Howard Taylor, *Borden of Yale* (Minneapolis: Bethany House, 1988).

[21] Geraldine Taylor, *Behind the Ranges: The Life-Changing Story of J. O. Fraser* (Littleton, CO: OMF Publications, 1998).

[22] Geraldine Taylor, *The Triumph of John and Betty Stam* (Chicago: Moody Publishers, 1935).

[23] In 1964, the China Inland Mission was renamed Overseas Missionary Fellowship, which was then shortened to OMF International.

[24] For how this can be computed from official statistics in China, see http://www.billionbibles.org/china/how-many-christians-in-china.html.

remove the scales from my eyes, and the Spirit of God revealed to me the truth of our oneness with Jesus as I had never known it before."[25]

Notice two things about that sentence. One is that the change in Taylor didn't come through new information. Taylor knew his Bible, and he knew what Keswick teachers were saying. Just that year, the magazine *Revival* had carried a series of articles by Robert Pearsall Smith on "the victorious life"[26]—one of the catchphrases of the Keswick teaching. These articles had been the inspiration for McCarthy's own experience that he was now sharing with Taylor. It was not a new teaching. It was one familiar sentence. We have all had experiences of this sort: the same truth we have read a hundred times explodes with new power in our lives. That happened for Taylor.

The other thing to notice is that the truth that exploded was his "oneness with Jesus." And Taylor says it carefully: "the Spirit of God revealed to me the truth of our oneness with Jesus *as I had never known it before*." He knew it before, but this time the Holy Spirit gave him a new sight of the wonder of it. This is exactly the way he understood it.

The prayer of Ephesians 1:18 was answered as never before: "having the eyes of your hearts enlightened, that you may know . . ." Taylor said: "As I read, I saw it all! . . . I looked to Jesus and saw (and when I saw, oh, how joy flowed!) that He had said, 'I will never leave thee.'"[27]

> I saw not only that Jesus will never leave me, but that I am a member of His body, of His flesh and of His bones. The vine is not the root merely, but all—root, stem, branches, twigs, leaves, flowers, fruit. And Jesus is not that alone—He is soil and sunshine, air and showers, and ten thousand times more than we have ever dreamed, wished for or needed. Oh, the joy of seeing this truth![28]

This was not new information. This was the miracle of the eyes of the heart being opened to taste and see at a deeper level than had been

25 Cited in Dr. and Mrs. Howard Taylor, *Hudson Taylor's Spiritual Secret*, 149.
26 Broomhall, *The Shaping of Modern China*, 109.
27 Cited in Dr. and Mrs. Howard Taylor, *Hudson Taylor's Spiritual Secret*, 149.
28 Cited in ibid., 149–50.

tasted and seen before. "Oh, taste and see that the LORD is good!" (Ps. 34:8). And the center of what he saw and tasted was union with Christ: "The sweetest part, if one may speak of one part being sweeter than another, is the rest which full *identification* with Christ brings."[29] The experience came to be known as the "exchanged life" because of Galatians 2:20: "I have been crucified with Christ. It is no longer I who live, but Christ who lives in me. And the life I now live in the flesh I live by faith in the Son of God, who loved me and gave himself for me."

Along with a new sight of Christ's fullness and his union with Christ, there was also a new yieldedness: "Surrender to Christ he had long known, but this was more; this was a new yieldedness, a glad, unreserved handing over of self and everything to Him."[30] This new yieldedness was so powerful and so sweet—so supernatural—that it rose up like an indictment against all vain striving. When you have been swept up into the arms of Jesus, all previous efforts to jump in seem vain.

At the heart of the discovery was this: the fruit of the vine comes from abiding, not striving:

> To let my loving Saviour work in me His will, my sanctification, is what I would live for by His grace. Abiding, not striving nor struggling; looking off unto Him; trusting Him for present power; resting in the love of an almighty Saviour.[31]

> From the consciousness of union springs the power to abide. Let us, then—not seek, not wait, not pursue—but now accept by faith the Saviour's word—"Ye *are* the branches."[32]

Taylor experienced such a powerful revelation of the inexpressible reality of union with Christ, as an absolute and glorious fact of security and sweetness and power, that it carried in it its own effectiveness.

---

[29] Cited in ibid. Italics added.
[30] Ibid., 154.
[31] Cited in ibid., 144.
[32] Cited in J. H. Taylor, *Hudson Taylor's Choice Sayings: A Compilation from His Writings and Addresses* (London: China Inland Mission, n.d.), 7.

It gave vivid meaning to the difference between the works of the flesh and the fruit of the Spirit: "Work is the outcome of effort; fruit, of life. A bad man may do good work, but a bad tree cannot bear good fruit."[33] "How to get faith strengthened? Not by striving after faith, but by resting on the Faithful One."[34]

Unlike many who claimed a higher-life experience, Taylor really was lifted to a plane of joy and peace and strength that lasted all his life. He wrote, "Never again did the unsatisfied days come back; never again was the needy soul separated from the fullness of Christ."[35] Just before turning sixty, Taylor was in Melbourne, Australia. An Episcopalian minister had heard of Keswick, and after spending time with Taylor, he wrote: "Here was the real thing, an embodiment of 'Keswick teaching' such as I had never hoped to see. It impressed me profoundly. Here was a man almost sixty years of age, bearing tremendous burdens, yet absolutely calm and untroubled."[36]

DECADES OF RESTING IN JESUS

Why did this crisis experience bear such lasting fruit for Hudson Taylor? There are at least three reasons.

1. Taylor was saturated with the Bible, and his interpretation of his experience was chastened by the Bible.

This means that in his experience, the walk of faith was not as passive as he made it sound. William Berger, Taylor's friend and the leader of the China Inland Mission in England, made plain to Taylor that he did not approve of "overstressing of the passive, receptive aspect of 'holiness.'"[37] He emphasized the need for active resistance to evil and of effort to obey God the way J. C. Ryle was to balance the Keswick Movement's emphases a few years later.[38]

---

[33] Cited in James Hudson Taylor, *A Ribband of Blue And Other Bible Studies*, Kindle edition (May 12, 2012), Locations 246–49.
[34] Cited in Dr. and Mrs. Howard Taylor, *Hudson Taylor's Spiritual Secret*, 149.
[35] Cited in ibid., 153.
[36] Cited in ibid., 215.
[37] Broomhall, *The Shaping of Modern China*, 111.
[38] See J. I. Packer's treatment of Ryle's view of sanctification and Ryle's own book, *Holiness*, in *Faithfulness and Holiness: The Witness of J. C. Ryle* (Wheaton, IL: Crossway, 2010).

Over the years, Taylor embraced this counsel, but never lost the wonder of being *really* united to the vine. He acknowledged: "Union is not identical with abiding: union is uninterrupted, but abiding may be interrupted. If abiding be interrupted, sin follows."[39] He not only recognized that abiding in Christ can be interrupted, leading to sin, but also that our best obedience needs cleansing: "We are sinful creatures, and our holiest service can only be accepted through Jesus Christ our Lord."[40]

His life was one resounding affirmation that God uses means to preserve and deepen and intensify our experience of union with Christ. These means are a kind of *effort*. To be sure, there are different kinds of effort. There is slavish effort and there is trusting effort—effort that leans on the flesh and effort that leans on God. "I worked harder than any of them, though it was not I, but the grace of God that is with me" (1 Cor. 15:10). "Whoever serves, [let him serve] as one who serves by the strength that God supplies" (1 Pet. 4:11). "The life I now live . . . I live by faith" (Gal. 2:20).

But in this *effort of faith* there are things to be done. In Taylor's own words: "Communion with Christ requires our coming to Him. Meditating upon His person and His work requires the diligent use of the means of grace, and specially the prayerful reading of His Word. Many fail to abide because they habitually fast instead of feed."[41] Taylor's new pattern was to go to bed earlier and then rise at five a.m. "to give time to Bible study and prayer (often two hours) before the work of the day began."[42]

---

[39] Cited in J. H. Taylor, *Hudson Taylor's Choice Sayings*, 1.

[40] Cited in J. H. Taylor, "Consecration and Blessing," in T. J. Shanks, ed., *College Students at Northfield; or, A College of Colleges, No. 2* (New York; Chicago: Revell, 1888), 78.

[41] Cited in J. H. Taylor, *Hudson Taylor's Choice Sayings*, 2.

[42] Dr. and Mrs. Howard Taylor, *Hudson Taylor's Spiritual Secret*, 145. One of the most moving scenes from his closing months is given by his son in describing how Taylor found time for prayer and the Word every day, no matter how busy: "To him, the secret of overcoming lay in daily, hourly fellowship with God; and this, he found, could only be maintained by secret prayer and feeding upon the Word through which He reveals Himself to the waiting soul. It was not easy for Mr Taylor, in his changeful life, to make time for prayer and Bible study, but he knew that it was vital. Well do the writers remember travelling with him month after month in northern China, by cart and wheelbarrow, with the poorest of inns at night. Often with only one large room for coolies and travellers alike, they would screen off a corner for their father and another for themselves, with curtains of some sort; and then, after sleep at last had brought a measure of quiet, they would hear a match struck and see the flicker of candlelight which told that Mr. Taylor, however weary, was poring over the little Bible in two volumes always at hand. From two to four A.M. was the time he usually gave to prayer; the time

Taylor never saw these disciplines in contradiction to his glorious experience of union with Christ. Jesus is the vine and his Father is the vinedresser. Both the power of the vine from within and the providence of the vinedresser from without serve the fullness of the experience of joy-filled, peace-filled, love-filled union with Christ.

2. The second reason Taylor's life-changing experience lasted was that he saw suffering as God's way of deepening and sweetening his experience of union with Christ.

The vinedresser does many things for the branches. But the one task Jesus focused on in John 15 was pruning or cutting. The aim of this is to preserve and intensify and make fruitful the branch's union with the vine. Taylor said:

> It is *only* in the trial of GOD's grace that its *beauty and power* can be seen. Then all our trials of temper, circumstances, provocation, sickness, disappointment, bereavement, will but give a higher burnish to the mirror, and enable us to reflect more fully and more perfectly the glory and blessedness of our MASTER.[43]

> It is in the path of obedience and self-denying service that God reveals Himself most intimately to His children. When it costs most we find the greatest joy. We find the darkest hours the brightest, and the greatest loss the highest gain. While the sorrow is short lived, and will soon pass away, the joy is far more exceeding, and it is eternal. Would that I could give you an idea of the way in which God has revealed Himself to me in China, and to others whom I have known. In the presence of bereavement, in the deepest sorrows of life, He has so drawn near to me that I have said to myself, Is it possible that the precious one who is in His presence can have more of the presence of God than I have?[44]

---

when he could be most sure of being undisturbed to wait upon God. That flicker of candlelight has meant more to them than all they have read or heard on secret prayer; it meant reality, not preaching but practice. The hardest part of a missionary career, Mr. Taylor found, is to maintain regular, prayerful Bible study. 'Satan will always find you something to do,' he would say, 'when you ought to be occupied about that, if it is only arranging a window blind.'" Cited in ibid., 223.

[43] Cited in J. H. Taylor, *Days of Blessing in Inland China: Being an Account of Meetings Held in the Province of Shan-Si, &c.*, 2nd ed. (London: Morgan & Scott, 1887), 61.

[44] Cited in *China's Millions*, No. 110, Vol. IX, August 1884, 102.

In other words, the experience of the fullness of union with Christ, with all its joy and peace and power and love, comes not only from the preciousness of the vine but also from the pruning of the vinedresser. God uses the means of pain as well as prayer and Bible reading. "All these difficulties," Taylor said, "are only platforms for the manifestation of His grace, power and love."[45]

3. Finally, his experience of sweet union with Christ lasted because he embraced the absolute goodness and sovereignty of God over his suffering and his union with Christ.

This is how Taylor could retain such composure in Christ in the most oppressive and dangerous and sorrowful and painful circumstances. He believed that the key to joy and peace and fruitfulness lay in being sure not only of the vine's all-satisfying sap, but also of the vinedresser's all-controlling sovereignty.

When he was fifty-two and confined to bed and feeling forgotten, he wrote, "So make up your mind that God is an infinite Sovereign, and has the right to do as He pleases with His own, and He may not explain to you a thousand things which may puzzle your reason in His dealings with you."[46] Taylor lost his wife Maria when she was thirty-three and he was thirty-eight. As noted in the introduction, he wrote to his mother, "From my inmost soul I delight in the knowledge that God does or permits all things, and causes all things to work together for good to those who love Him."[47]

Though Satan is real and causes much evil in the world, Taylor was strengthened by the assurance that God never loses control: "Oftentimes shall we be helped and blessed if we bear this in mind—that Satan is servant, and not master, and that he, and wicked men incited by him, are only permitted to do that which GOD by His determinate counsel and foreknowledge has before determined shall be done."[48]

---

[45] Cited in Dr. and Mrs. Howard Taylor, *Hudson Taylor's Spiritual Secret*, 202. "The highest service demands the greatest sacrifice, but it secures the fullest blessing and the greatest fruitfulness." *The Works of J. Hudson Taylor* (Douglas Editions, 2009), Kindle edition, Location 2955.
[46] Cited in Jim Cromarty, *It Is Not Death to Die* (Fearn, Ross-shire, Scotland: Christian Focus, 2008), 8.
[47] Cited in Dr. and Mrs. Howard Taylor, *Hudson Taylor's Spiritual Secret*, 163.
[48] Cited in James Hudson Taylor, *A Ribband of Blue And Other Bible Studies*, Locations 375–76.

In other words, the vinedresser may use anything and anyone he pleases to prune the branch that he loves (John 15:1–2).

CONCLUSION

So I conclude that, while the Keswick teaching may in many cases have overemphasized the passivity of the pursuit of holiness and may have overemphasized a distinct crisis experience of consecration as the means of entering the "higher life," nevertheless Hudson Taylor's life bears witness to the possibility of living with more peace and more joy and more fruit in hardship than most of us enjoy.

Paul said he had learned this secret:

> I have learned in whatever situation I am to be content. I know how to be brought low, and I know how to abound. In any and every circumstance, I have learned the secret of facing plenty and hunger, abundance and need. I can do all things through him who strengthens me. (Phil. 4:11–13)

The learning is both *information* and *realization*. The *information* is the truth of Scripture that the vine is infinitely sufficient and satisfying for our souls' hunger, and that the vinedresser is all-controlling in care for the branches. And the *realization* is the miracle of actually resting in this truth, actually experiencing Christ and the Father becoming for us experientially all that they are.

Whether God gives you a crisis moment of this realization that lasts a lifetime, as he did Hudson Taylor, or leads you deeper gradually over time, don't settle for anything less than what Paul experienced in Philippians 4 and what he prayed for in Ephesians 3:19—that we might be "filled with all the fullness of God." Don't stop wanting this fullness and pursuing it.

If Hudson Taylor were here, he would say: "It is yours in Christ. Possess it. Enjoy it. Who knows? God may birth a ministry through you that lasts 150 years."

If his glory will come of it, shall I not even crave the honour of being the agent of his glory, even though it be by lying passive and enduring in anguish.

Charles Spurgeon

The Lord will give me the necessaries of life, if I first seek the kingdom of God and His righteousness: for there is a promise to that effect. Matthew 6:33.

George Müller

Let us see that we keep God before our eyes; that we walk in His ways, and seek to please and glorify Him in everything, great and small. Depend upon it, God's work done in God's way will never lack God's supplies.

Hudson Taylor

CONCLUSION

Perhaps the most striking and uniting thread in the interwoven lives of Charles Spurgeon, George Müller, and Hudson Taylor was their great confidence that God could and would fulfill all his promises of care to each of his children. And it follows, they believed, that all of us who, through Christ, know God as our heavenly Father should trust him implicitly to fulfill those promises very specifically and practically for us in our daily lives. And, they believed, our aim in that practical faith should be that God would be glorified through his Son as an all-powerful, all-wise, all-loving, promise-keeping God for those who trust him. Theirs was a camaraderie of confidence in the goodness, glory, and power of God.

This confidence was based on explicit promises in the Bible that, they believed, it would be sin not to believe:

- "Seek first the kingdom of God and his righteousness, and all these things will be added to you" (Matt. 6:33).
- "The LORD God is a sun and shield; the LORD bestows favor and honor. No good thing does he withhold from those who walk uprightly" (Ps. 84:11).
- "And we know that for those who love God all things work together for good, for those who are called according to his purpose" (Rom. 8:28).
- "Oh, fear the LORD, you his saints, for those who fear him have no lack!" (Ps. 34:9).

Each of these promises is conditional: seek the kingdom; walk uprightly; love God; fear the Lord. Taylor clarified for us that this does not mean that we must be perfect in order to enjoy these promises:

"No good thing will He withhold from them that walk uprightly."
Not, "from them that walk perfectly, or sinlessly"—no one does
that; not, "from them that are blameless"—though we all should
be that; but if we are honestly and uprightly seeking to serve Him,
no good thing will He withhold. What a rich promise this is![1]

Indeed, it is rich. It is staggeringly rich. It means we will always have
what we *need* if we trust him and walk uprightly. These three friends
did not believe God had promised that we will always have what we
want. Nor did they believe that God had promised to spare them suffering and death. "There is no promise to that effect. . . . [Rather] the
Lord will give me the necessaries of life, if I first seek the kingdom
of God and His righteousness: for there is a promise to that effect.
Matt. vi."[2]

Thus, when Paul says, "My God will supply every need of yours
according to his riches in glory in Christ Jesus" (Phil. 4:19), they understood "need" the way Paul does a few verses earlier:

Not that I am speaking of being in *need*, for I have learned in whatever situation I am to be content. I know how to be brought low,
and I know how to abound. In any and every circumstance, I have
learned the secret of facing plenty and hunger, abundance and *need*.
I can do all things through him who strengthens me. (vv. 11–13)

Paul says he always has what he *needs*—which includes times of being
"brought low" and times of being in "hunger" and "need." In other
words, Paul has no need when he is in need! He has no need when
he is in hunger.

What does that mean? It means that Paul puts Jesus Christ and his
glory above all earthly needs, and says, "If Christ is with me, and if
Christ is my supreme treasure, and if Christ is deciding what is good
for me, then I am content with what he decides, and have no needs."

---

[1] J. Hudson Taylor, *A Ribband of Blue and Other Bible Studies* (Toronto: China Inland Mission, n.d.), 107–8.
[2] George Müller, *A Narrative of Some of the Lord's Dealing with George Muller, Written by Himself, Jehovah Magnified. Addresses by George Muller Complete and Unabridged*, vol. 1 (Muskegon, MI: Dust and Ashes Publications, 2003), 65.

Whatever gain I had, I counted as loss for the sake of Christ. Indeed, I count everything as loss because of the surpassing worth
of knowing Christ Jesus my Lord. For his sake I have suffered the
loss of all things and count them as rubbish, in order that I may
gain Christ. (vv. 7–8)

The glory of God was always the preeminent issue in the life of faith
for Spurgeon, Müller, and Taylor. If God should will that the time for
their death had come, they would say with Paul, "It is my eager expec-
tation and hope that . . . Christ will be honored in my body, whether
by life or by death" (Phil. 1:20). They would not think the promises of
God's care had failed. What would it mean in this situation that God
"withholds no good thing"? It would mean that he did not withhold
the grace to die in a way that would magnify Christ. This was the
greatest "need" they felt.

Thus Spurgeon spoke of his own suffering. If it served the glory
of God according to God's will, then suffering was his desire—not
his physical pleasure, to be sure, but his deepest desire. His deepest
"need," which would not be withheld from him, was that God be
glorified in his life and death:

Moreover, we should not only bear all things because the Lord
ordains them, but because he orders all things for a wise, kind,
beneficent purpose. He doth not afflict willingly. He takes no delight in the sufferings of his children. Whenever adversity must
come it is always with a purpose; and, if a purpose of God is to be
subserved by my suffering, would I wish to escape from it? If his
glory will come of it, shall I not even crave the honour of being
the agent of his glory, even though it be by lying passive and enduring in anguish.[3]

Therefore, the camaraderie of confidence in God that these friends
shared did not include the confidence that they would never get sick

---

[3] C. H. Spurgeon, *The Metropolitan Tabernacle Pulpit Sermons*, vol. 22 (London: Passmore & Alabaster, 1876), 38.

or that they would be able to pray their loved ones out of the hospital. Both Müller and Taylor laid two wives in their graves because of illness. They both lost children. And Spurgeon died early because of a body wracked with disease.

Their confidence was not that God would prevent sickness and death, but that God would give them all they needed to do his will and give him glory in life and death. Taylor famously said, "Depend upon it, God's work done in God's way will never lack God's supplies."[4] This is a paraphrase of 2 Corinthians 9:8: "God is able to make all grace abound to you, so that having all sufficiency in all things at all times, you may abound in every good work." What does "every good work" mean? It does not refer to the "good works" required of someone else on the other side of the world. Rather, it refers to the works God is calling you to do today. Thus, Taylor expanded his motto: "The Lord does not require anything outside of that which He has given to His people, to accomplish His present purposes, whatever they may be."[5]

Nor should we leave the life stories of this book thinking that Müller and Taylor chose their particular strategy of trusting God, without asking people for help, because it was the only obedient way. They did not believe it was sin to ask someone for help. Müller made it clear that his way was not for everyone. He chose it because it seemed to him that this was God's way for him to put God's glory most clearly on display:

> I do not mean to say that it would be acting against the precepts of the Lord to seek for help in His work by personal and individual application to believers, (though it would be in direct opposition to His will to apply to unbelievers, 2 Cor. vi. 14–18); but I act in the way in which I do for the benefit of the Church at large, cheerfully bearing the trials, and sometimes the deep trials connected with this life of faith (which however brings along with it also its pre-

---

[4] J. H. Taylor, *Hudson Taylor's Choice Sayings: A Compilation from His Writings and Addresses* (London: China Inland Mission, n.d.), 65.
[5] Ibid., 60.

cious joys), if by any means a part at least of my fellow believers might be led to see the reality of dealing with God only, and that there is such a thing as the child of God having power with God by prayer and faith.[6]

This was the great aim—that people might "be led *to see*." To see the glory of God. To see his power, his wisdom, his care, his readiness to answer prayer, and his absolute commitment to meet every need we have, as we trust in him. Spurgeon and Müller would all rejoice to say "Amen" to these words of Hudson Taylor:

> In the greatest difficulties, in the heaviest trials, in the deepest poverty and necessities, He has never failed me; but, because I was enabled by His grace to trust in Him, He has always appeared for my help. I delight in speaking well of His Name.[7]

These three swans are not silent. Their lives and their words to this day are "speaking well of His name." And I delight to put the modest megaphone of this book to their lips. They would be glad, I think (in their very practical bent!), if we end on Taylor's own note of exhortation, full of hope:

> Let us see that we keep God before our eyes; that we walk in His ways, and seek to please and glorify Him in everything, great and small. Depend upon it, God's work done in God's way will never lack God's supplies.[8]

---

[6] Müller, *A Narrative*, 1:322 (emphasis added).
[7] Cited in Frederick Howard Taylor and Geraldine Taylor, *Hudson Taylor and the China Inland Mission: The Growth of a Work of God* (Littleton, CO; Mississauga, ON; Kent, TN: OMF Book, 1995), 183.
[8] J. H. Taylor, *Hudson Taylor's Choice Sayings*, 65.

INDEX OF SCRIPTURES

Psalms
34:8 — 98
34:9 — 105
84:11 — 72, 105
119:68 — 68

Isaiah
46:10 — 49

Jeremiah
1:12 — 49

Matthew
6 — 106
6:33 — 72, 104, 105

John
4:14 — 93
15 — 101
15:1–2 — 103

Acts
14:22 — 37

Romans
8:28 — 105
13:8 — 25, 26, 64

1 Corinthians
3:6 — 96
9:22 — 13
12:9 — 69, 71
15:10 — 34, 58, 100

2 Corinthians
1:6 — 43
3:18 — 57

4:12 — 43
4:16–18 — 55
6:14–18 — 108
9:8 — 108

Galatians
2:20 — 98, 100

Ephesians
1:18 — 97
3:16–19 — 86
3:19 — 103
5:18–19 — 86

Philippians
1:9 — 86
1:20 — 107
3:12 — 43
3:20 — 13
4 — 103
4:7 — 87
4:7–8 — 107
4:11–13 — 103, 106
4:19 — 87, 106

Colossians
1:24 — 43
1:29 — 42

1 Thessalonians
4:1 — 86
4:9–10 — 86

1 Peter
1:2 — 86
2:11 — 13
4:11 — 100

Index of Persons

Ahithophel, 34
Alleine, Joseph, 36
Amundsen, Darrel W., 45, 47, 48, 49, 50, 55
Apollos, 58
Augustine, 9
Austin, Alvyn, 10, 16, 17, 23, 24, 27, 88, 90

Baxter, Richard, 36, 56
Bebbington, David W., 9, 13, 15, 16, 17, 18, 19, 22, 23, 25
Bell, Alexander Graham, 16
Berger, William Thomas, 20, 99
Bergin, G. Fred, 24, 66
Borden, William, 96
Broomhall, A. J., 20, 94, 97, 99
Brown, Peter, 9
Bunyan, John, 36

Carey, William, 74
Cephas, 58
Champness, Thomas, 26
Covell, Ralph R., 96
Cromarty, Jim, 31, 102

Dallimore, Arnold, 21, 39, 42
Darby, John Nelson, 20
Darwin, Charles, 17
David, 48
Demas, 34
Dickens, Charles, 19
Dyer, Maria, 91

Earl of Shaftesbury, 42
Edison, Thomas, 16

Elliff, Jim, 10
Eraclius, 9

Faulding, Jennie, 95
Fraser, James, 96
Fung, Patrick, 96

George, Christian, 10
Groves, Mary, 67
Guinness, Grattan, 20
Guinness, M. G., 91

Haley, Bruce, 16
Hardey, Robert, 20, 90
Hayden, Eric W., 27, 36, 37, 38, 42, 52
Haykin, Michael, 10
Hill, Richard, 20
Hillyard, Mrs., 35
Holden, J. Stuart, 30
Howard family, 20
Hulse, Erroll, 22, 38, 39, 40, 41, 45, 46, 47, 48, 54
Hutson, Curtis, 45

Jacob (patriarch), 88
James, John Angell, 36
John the Baptist, 51

Kingdon, David, 22, 38, 39, 40, 41, 45, 46, 47, 54

Lae-djün, Wang, 26, 88
Livingstone, David, 42
Lord Palmerston, 15
Lord Shaftesbury, 21

Luther, Martin, 27

Mathis, David, 11
McCarthy, John, 96
McKay, Moira, 23
Mill, John Stuart, 17
Moody, D. L., 63
Müller, Elijah, 67
Müller, George, 9, 10, 11, 12, 13, 14,
    15, 17, 18, 19, 20, 21, 22, 23, 24,
    25, 26, 27, 28, 29, 30, 31, 35, 37,
    59, 62, 63–83, 90, 91, 104, 105,
    106, 107, 108, 109
Müller, Lydia, 67
Müller, Mary, 67–69, 72, 82
Murray, Iain H., 46

Naselli, Andy, 85
Nettles, Thomas, 10, 35
Nicol, Lewis, 92
Noll, Mark, 10

Orr, J. Edwin, 17
Owen, John, 53

Packer, J. I., 99
Parker, Joseph, 47
Paul (apostle), 37, 40, 43, 50, 55, 103
Pierson, A. T., 24, 63, 64, 65, 66, 67,
    80
Piper, Noël, 11
Pollock, John, 96

Queen Victoria, 15

Reinke, Tony, 10
Ross, Bob L., 41
Ryle, J. C., 99

Sangar, Susannah, 67
Scroggie, William, 85

Segal, Marshall, 11
Shanks, T. J., 100
Simpson, James, 45
Smith, Hannah, 87
Smith, Robert, 87, 97
Spurgeon, Charles, 9, 10, 11, 12, 13,
    14, 17, 18, 19, 21, 22, 23, 25, 27,
    28, 29, 30, 31, 32, 33–60, 63, 74,
    88, 89, 90, 104, 105, 107, 108, 109
Spurgeon, Charles Jr., 35, 38
Spurgeon, Susannah, 45
Spurgeon, Thomas, 35
Stafford, Tim, 56, 57
Stam, Betty, 96
Stam, John, 96
Stead, Louisa M. R., 88

Taylor, Amelia, 90
Taylor, Dr. and Mrs. Howard, 31, 91,
    92, 93, 97, 98, 99, 100, 102
Taylor, Frederick Howard, 20, 21, 87,
    93, 109
Taylor, Geraldine, 20, 21, 87, 93, 96,
    106, 109
Taylor, Howard, 96
Taylor, Hudson, 9, 10, 11, 12, 13, 14,
    16, 17, 18, 20, 21, 22, 23, 24, 25,
    26, 27, 28, 29, 30, 31, 59, 63, 84,
    85–103, 104, 105, 107, 108, 109
Taylor, J. H., 91, 92, 94, 98, 99, 100,
    101, 102, 106, 108, 109
Taylor, Maria, 30, 88, 92, 94, 95, 102
Taylor, Noel, 94
Taylor, Samuel, 94
Thompson, Susannah, 35

Walls, Andrew, 14
Watts, Isaac, 36
Wells, James, 47
Wesley, John, 18
Wolffe, John, 9
Wright, James, 67

Index of Subjects

activism, 18–19, 21, 30, 33–35, 44–48
affliction, 50
age of invention, 15
"Alleine's Alarm," 36
The Anxious Inquirer (James), 36

Baptist Union, 47
biography, 9, 11
Boxer Rebellion, 95
Bright's disease, 37, 45–46

Call to the Unconverted (Baxter), 36
Calvinist/Calvinism, 30, 40–41, 47, 63, 74, 78–80
Cambridge Seven, 96
China Inland Mission, 13, 16, 23, 24, 25, 26, 28, 91–92, 95, 99
Chinese Evangelisation Society, 25, 90
Christ, 81
  beauty of, 21
  identification with, 98
  incarnation of, 13–14
  satisfaction with, 68–69
  sovereign triumph of, 59–60
  transformation, 13–14
  union with, 85, 87, 96–99, 100
Christian Advocate, 18
Christianity, 14
Christianity Today, 56
Commenting on Commentaries (Spurgeon), 42
Communion with God (Owen), 53
creation
  beauty of, 21
criticism, 37, 56, 58
Cultural Revolution, 95

debt, 25–28, 90–91
depression, 48, 49–51
Downgrade Controversy, 47, 56, 58

entrepreneurialism, 23
eternity, 55
evangelicalism, 17–18
exiles on earth, 13

faith, 29
  gift of, 69–72
  grace of, 69–72

God
  conditional promises of, 105–9
  confidence in, 105–9
  glory of, 11, 29, 40, 107
  goodness of, 11, 51
  happiness in, 80–83
  power of, 11
  seeking to be happy in, 78–80
  sovereign goodness of, 73–75
  sovereignty of, 49, 77–78, 83
grace, 68
  doctrines of, 74–75
  strategies of, 49, 51, 53, 55–56, 56–59, 59–60
Grace Abounding (Bunyan), 36
Great Awakening(s), 9–10, 16–17, 63
Great Exhibition, 15

healing, 72
"higher life," 99, 103

indigenizing principle, 14
individualism, 22–23, 30

Industrial Revolution, 15
introspection, 34

John Ploughman's Talk (Spurgeon), 42
justification, 14

Keswick Movement/teaching, 85, 86,
    87, 93, 97, 99, 103

Logos Bible Software, 11
loss, 37

meditation, 53–55
Methodist(s), 16–17
Metropolitan Tabernacle, 27, 35, 36,
    41, 88
money, 69–72, 75–77
    not asking people for, 28–30
Morning and Evening (Spurgeon), 42

nature, 51–53
New Park Street Chapel, 35, 36, 37

OMF International, 96
On Liberty (Mills), 17
On the Origin of Species (Darwin), 17
orphan care, 19–21, 65, 69–71
    reasons for establishing orphan
        houses, 29
Our Own Hymnbook (Spurgeon), 42
Overseas Missionary Fellowship, 96

pain, 54–55
Pastors' College (Spurgeon), 34, 37,
    41
pilgrim principle, 14
The Pilgrim's Progress (Bunyan), 36
Plymouth Brethren, 20, 35
pragmatism, 30

prayer, 21, 29, 53–55, 75–77
preaching, 33–35, 66
    Bible-believing, 39
    of Spurgeon, 36–48
    truth-driven, 38
Primitive Methodist Church, 36
Protestantism, 40
Puritan morality, 41
Puritanism, 40
Puritans, 36

rest, 51–53
ridicule, 46

sacrifice, 79
salvation, 39–40
sanctification, 14, 56–57, 85
Scripture, 81–83, 99–101
Scripture Knowledge Institution for
    Home and Abroad, 23–25, 64
self-denial, 79
self-indulgence, 18
sickness, 37, 45
    as blessing, 49
slander, 46
sorrow, 37
Stockwell Orphanage, 35
suffering, 30, 44–48, 101–3, 107–8
The Sword and the Trowel, 35

Treasury of David (Spurgeon), 42

University of Halle, 72, 73

wellness, 43
Wesleyan Methodists, 89, 90
work, 42–44

zeal, 43

✳ desiringGod

Everyone wants to be happy. Our website was born and built for happiness. We want people everywhere to understand and embrace the truth that *God is most glorified in us when we are most satisfied in him*. We've collected more than thirty years of John Piper's speaking and writing, including translations into more than forty languages. We also provide a daily stream of new written, audio, and video resources to help you find truth, purpose, and satisfaction that never end. And it's all available free of charge, thanks to the generosity of people who've been blessed by the ministry.

If you want more resources for true happiness, or if you want to learn more about our work at Desiring God, we invite you to visit us at www.desiringGod.org.

www.desiringGod.org

Each book in The Swans Are Not Silent series focuses
on three renowned leaders from church history,
offering a close look at the course of their individual
lives and their impact on our own spirituality today.

THE LEGACY OF SOVEREIGN JOY
Augustine, Martin Luther, John Calvin

THE HIDDEN SMILE OF GOD
John Bunyan, William Cowper, David Brainerd

THE ROOTS OF ENDURANCE
John Newton, Charles Simeon, William Wilberforce

CONTENDING FOR OUR ALL
Athanasius, John Owen, J. Gresham Machen

FILLING UP THE AFFLICTIONS OF CHRIST
William Tyndale, Adoniram Judson, John Paton

SEEING BEAUTY AND SAYING BEAUTIFULLY
George Herbert, George Whitefield, C. S. Lewis

For more information, visit crossway.org.